Tell Me Honey...2000 Questions for Couples

Tell Me Honey…2000 Questions for Couples

Vikram Chandiramani

The official website of this book is http://www.tellmehoney.com

First Published in India in 2010 by VMC Infotech
Printed in Charleston, South Carolina, USA

VMC Infotech
222/ Shantivan,
New Link Rd. Extn.,
Andheri West
Mumbai 53, India
Tel: 91-22-66996298
Fax: 91-22-26350503

ISBN-13: 978-1451501896

First Edition: March 2010

These questions are a result of hundreds of conversations, over many years with all the girls I have known and who have touched my life in some way. I'm richer for the experience and I dedicate this book to them.

Contents

Preface

If you hate reading, but have been attracted to this book, here's the good news - this book isn't meant to be read cover to cover. Just dip into it at any point, find a question and ask your partner!

You'll be able to know about your partner's hopes, desires, ambitions, romantic inclinations, relationship skills, sexual needs, childhood, work and career priorities, fears, complexes, apprehensions, values, money priorities, family goals, talents and skills, addictions, beliefs and convictions, self image and a lot else that you would probably never have discovered.

You'll find these questions useful, irrespective of your current situation. If you're single and looking, many of these questions can help you start and carry on an interesting conversation with a potential partner. You'll be able to know whether you share values, life goals and are on the same wavelength. You'll begin to see how your partner approaches relationships.

If you're already in a relationship and want to know your partner better, these questions can help you know more and more about your partner each day. You'll be able to nurture your relationship and grow together, in every way. Even if you've been married for several years, you're almost certain to discover new aspects to your spouse's personality, with these questions.

If you're going to invest precious years of your life in a relationship, then this book will prove to be an invaluable tool in knowing whether you're spending your time on a person who's 'right' for you. I wish someone had given it to me when I started dating!

A few things to keep in mind:

- ✓ There are no right answers or wrong answers to these questions. Every answer provides you an insight into your partner.
- ✓ Try not to be overly judgmental when asking these questions. Make it a fun way to explore each other's personality. Don't hold any of the answers against your partner.
- ✓ Don't ask too many questions at once, especially if you're in a new relationship. That can intimidate some people.
- ✓ Some of these questions are excellent for 'get acquainted' dates. Others are best suited for lovers or spouses wanting to get closer. Use your judgment.

Do visit tellmehoney.com to join my mailing list so I can keep you informed about my forthcoming books. You can also buy more copies of this book at a discount to gift to your friends.

1

Addictions

1. Are you addicted to any prescription drugs?

2. Are you addicted to anything?

3. At what age did you start drinking?

4. At what age did you start smoking?

5. Do you drink? Which alcoholic drink do you prefer the most?

6. Do you smoke?

7. Have you ever taken drugs?

8. Have you ever tried to quit alcohol? Did it work? Do you think you could ever give it up?

9. Have you ever tried to quit smoking? Was it difficult to do so?

10. How many cigarettes a day do you smoke?

11. If your smoking bothers someone, do you stub out your cigarette?

12. When was the first time you tried a cigarette? How old were you? What made you try it?

13. When was the first time you tried alcohol? How old were you? What made you try it?

14. Which is the one habit you would like to break?

2

Adventure

15. Are you adventurous?

16. Do you like dare-devil activities?

17. Do you like trying out new restaurants?

18. Have you ever been part of a nudist club or camp?

19. Have you ever gone backpacking?

20. Have you ever got a tattoo done? Where on your body is it?

21. Have you ever played strip poker?

22. Have you ever tried mood altering drugs?

23. Is there anything you have always wanted to do but have been afraid to?

24. What is the biggest risk you have ever taken?

25. What is the craziest thing you have ever done?

26. Which is the most dangerous situation you've ever been in?

3

Ambitions

27. Do you think everyday responsibilities come in the way of your reaching for and achieving higher goals?

28. Do you think you are capable of running your own business?

29. Have you ever wanted to write a book?

30. How ambitious are you?

31. If a venture capital fund or a bank, was willing to finance any business that you started, what would it be?

32. If you were trying to attain a professional ambition, but kept failing at it, how long would you keep trying before giving up?

33. Is there any ambition you think you wouldn't be able to pursue, if you married me?

34. What are the goals for your life?

35. What are the goals you have set for yourself?

36. What are your goals for the year ahead?

37. What is the one possession you hope to acquire some day?

38. What is the one thing you feel you must do in your lifetime, without which you would be very disappointed at the end of your life?

39. What would you want people to remember you as?

40. Which goals did you set for yourself when you completed your education? Do you think you have achieved them?

41. Would you like to be world famous or would you resent leading a 'goldfish-in-a-fishbowl' existence?

42. Would you rather have a predictable and comfortable life, or a life full of adventure and ups and downs - great heights and depths?

4

Anger

43. Have you ever been in a brawl?

44. How do you deal with anger?

45. If you could kill any one person by just wishing it, who would that be?

46. When was the last time you lost your temper?

5

Animals and Pets

47. Are you emotionally attached to your pets?

48. Do you like animals and birds?

49. Do you spend a lot of time taking care of your pets?

50. Do you take your pets with you when you go travelling? If not, who takes care of them in your absence?

51. Have you ever brought a stray dog or other animal home or otherwise cared for them?

52. Have you ever gone hunting? What did you hunt?

53. Have you ever lost a pet?

54. Have you ever lost a pet? How did you cope with the loss?

55. How much of an animal lover are you?

56. If you were a pet lover and married someone who couldn't stand pets, how would you deal with this?

57. If your neighbors made a police complaint against your pet, what would you do?

58. What are your views about drug testing on animals?

59. What sort of pets have you kept over the years?

60. When was the last time you visited a zoo? Do you like animals?

61. Would you have a pet spayed or neutered?

6

Art and Culture

62. Are there any specific painters or sculptors whose work you admire?

63. Are you interested in antiques?

64. Are you interested in art and paintings?

65. Do you like theatre and drama? Which genre of theatre do you prefer?

66. How often do you attend concerts?

67. How often do you go to the museum?

68. Is there any culture you're particularly fascinated by?

69. What sort of art do you like?

70. Which are the cultures, other than your own, that you've seen closely?

7

Beliefs and Convictions

71. Are there any causes you feel very strongly about?

72. Do you believe in UFOs?

73. Do you believe in voodoo or black magic?

74. Do you think there is a purpose for everything that happens?

75. How much of a role do you think luck plays in our lives?

76. How superstitious are you?

77. Some people follow astrology to determine auspicious times before they do anything. What you think of this?

78. What do you think is the purpose of your life?

79. What is your lucky color?

80. What is your lucky number?

81. Which of your personal convictions or beliefs would you never compromise on?

82. What do you think of vegans, who don't drink milk, because they believe it rightfully belongs to the calf?

8

Birthdays

83. Do birthdays depress you because they bring the realization that you're growing older?

84. Do you look forward to getting birthday gifts?

85. Do you look forward to your birthday?

86. Does it bother you if someone forgets to wish you on your birthday?

87. Does your birthday make you happy?

88. Has anyone ever thrown a surprise birthday party for you?

89. Have you ever thrown a surprise birthday party for anyone?

90. How did you celebrate your birthday in your childhood? How do you celebrate it now?

91. How many people wish you on your birthday?

92. When is your birthday?

9

Cars and Driving

93. Are you part of a car pool?

94. Are you possessive about your car/bike? Would you let a family member or a friend borrow it?

95. Can you drive a car? Do you like driving? Do you like cars?

96. Can you fix minor problems in your car, yourself?

97. Do you consider it absolutely essential to have a car?

98. Do you consider yourself a safe driver?

99. Do you generally overtake other cars when you drive?

100. Do you know how to ride a motorcycle?

101. Do you own a car?

102. Do you prefer to drive or be driven?

103. Do you talk on the cell phone when driving?

104. Do you think you are a competent driver?

105. Do you usually buy a car cash down, or do you prefer taking a loan and paying installments?

106. Do you wear a helmet when riding a motorcycle?

107. Do you wear seat belts when driving a car?

108. How frequently do you wash your car? Do you wash it yourself or get it done at a car wash?

109. How much time do you spend looking after your car/bike every week?

110. How often do you change your car?

111. How often do you get a ticket or have to pay a fine for your driving or for parking?

112. How possessive are you about your car?

113. If your partner asked you to drive at a slower pace, how would you react?

114. If you're not able to find your way when driving, how likely are you to ask for directions?

115. Which is your dream car?

116. Which was the first car you owned?

117. Which was your first car?

10

Charity

118. Are you associated with any non-profit organizations?

119. Are you into charity?

120. Do you ever give alms to beggars? Do you see this as supporting the act of begging, when the focus could instead be on making them self-sufficient?

121. Have you ever donated blood?

122. Have you pledged to donate your organs when you die?

123. Which causes do you believe in?

11

Childhood

124. After your younger siblings came along, was there a sense of jealousy and competition?

125. As a child, who would you turn to, when you had something to ask?

126. As a teenager, which posters adorned the walls of your room?

127. Did you ever get into any major trouble, as a child? Tell me about it.

128. Did you ever run away from home? Did you ever seriously consider doing so?

129. Did you have a nickname in school?

130. Did you have a teacher in school, who was always picking on you?

131. Did you like going to school? If yes, what did you like about it? If not, why not?

132. Did you witness your parents' quarrelling, when you were a child? How did it affect you?

133. Do you remember your first day of school?

134. How much pocket money did you get as a child?

135. How was your relationship with your parents, when growing up?

136. If you could relive your childhood, what would you change about it?

137. Is there anyone from your childhood, you would like to meet again?

138. Is there anything you were always hauled up, for as a teen?

139. Was there any particularly trying phase in your childhood?

140. Was there anyone who, looking back, was a negative influence on you, during your growing up years?

141. Were you ever punished in school? What was it like?

142. Were you ever teased about anything in school?

143. Were you jealous of any of your classmates or friends in school?

144. Were you perceived as being a trouble maker in school?

145. Were you popular in high school?

146. Were you the studious sort, in school?

147. Were your friends perceived as 'bad company' by your parents?

148. What did you wish and pray for, as a child?

149. What do you like or dislike about the places where you grew up?

150. What is your earliest memory of childhood?

151. What sort of friends did you have in school?

152. What sort of sports and activities did you participate in, when in school?

153. What was Halloween like, when you were a child?

154. What was the home like, where you spend your childhood?

155. What was your childhood like?

156. What were you like, as a teenager?

157. What were you like, as a child?

158. Which are the talents you had as a child, that your parents encouraged you to develop?

159. Which city were you born in?

160. Which comics or books did you read as a child?

161. Which has been your most memorable Halloween costume?

162. Which subject did you find the toughest in school? Do you still have to struggle with it?

163. Which subjects did you love, in school? Which ones did you hate?

164. Which was your best year in school?

165. Which were your favorite toys, in childhood?

166. Who was the strongest positive influence on you, during your childhood?

167. Who was your childhood crush?

168. Who was your first prom date?

169. Who was your hero, as a child?

12

Children

170. Are there any names you have thought of, for your children?

171. At what age would you allow your kids to start dating?

172. Do children lose their innocence much earlier now, due to the wide exposure to various media?

173. Do you expect your kids to do household chores, or help around the house?

174. Do you like children?

175. Do you like to include your children in your holiday celebrations?

176. Do you see yourself being liberal with your children, or a strict disciplinarian?

177. Do you think children grow up too fast these days?

178. Do you think girls and boys need to be brought up in a different manner? How?

179. Do you think going to a finishing school is important?

180. Do you think pets become substitutes for children?

181. Do you think that when both parents work, the children don't get enough time and attention?

182. Do you think that when full-time-motherhood was the norm, children were better brought up and crime was lower?

183. Do you think you would be a good role model for your children?

184. Have you ever stayed in a hostel, during your school days?

185. How easy or difficult is it to bring up children, according to you?

186. How financially stable would you want to be, before you decide to have children?

187. How important do you think it is for kids, to learn the value of money?

188. How important is it that your kids be well mannered? How would you teach them manners and etiquette?

189. How important is it to you, that your child tops his class in school?

190. How important is it to you, that your kids be disciplined?

191. How many children would you like to have?

192. How much money would make you feel secure to start a family?

193. How much of a role do you think the mother should personally play, in bringing up a child?

194. How much pocket money would you give your children today?

195. How much time would you devote, to bringing up your children?

196. How would you demonstrate your affection for your children?

197. How would you express anger to your children? Would you beat or spank them?

198. If we could never have children, how would you deal with it? Would it change our relationship in any way?

199. If we could never have children, would you consider adopting a child?

200. If you could choose the gender of an unborn child, would you do it?

201. If you could customize the features of an unborn child with genetics, would you do it?

202. If you found out that your son was gay, or your daughter was a lesbian, how would you deal with it?

203. If you were unable to get pregnant due to health issues, would you be open to having a surrogate mother?

204. If you were unable to impregnate me due to health issues, would you be willing for us to opt for a sperm donor?

205. If your kid was the violent sort, how would you deal with it?

206. What advice would you give your kids to protect them from paedophiles?

207. What do you think of bringing kids into a world like this one?

208. What do you think of daycare for children?

209. What sort of education would you want your children to have?

210. What sort of qualities would you want your children to inherit from you?

211. Which are the values that you would like your family and children to uphold?

212. Which areas of your children's lives do you see yourself having a major role in?

213. Which aspects of child rearing do you think mothers should delegate to a nanny, if they can afford one?

214. Which qualities of mine and your own would you like our children to have?

215. Which school would you want to send your children to?

216. Would you attend child birth classes, if your wife was pregnant?

217. Would you be open to being a step-parent?

218. Would you change the diapers of your baby?

219. Would you delay starting a family, until you are financially more secure?

220. Would you like to have children someday?

221. Would you like to have male or female children?

222. Would you play a role in helping your children with their studies?

223. Would you send your kids to a finishing school?

224. Would you send your kids to a hostel, to study?

225. Would you want to decide or influence the career choices of your children?

226. Would you want to spoil or pamper your children?

227. Would you want your children to be religious?

228. Would you want your children to be vegetarians?

229. Would you want your children to grow up to be like you?

230. What would you do if your child was caught stealing in school.

231. How would you deal with your child putting on too much weight.

232. If your children asked you to give up smoking because they were educated about passive smoking in school, how would you react?

233. If your kid told you about someone at school who was touching him/her improperly what would you do?

234. If you found that your child was feigning illness regularly to miss school, how would you deal with this?

235. If the people at school told you that your kid was missing classes all the time, how would you handle this?

236. What would you do if your teenaged son or daughter joined a cult?

237. If your ten year old asked you about sex, what would you say?

238. Your child insisted on an expensive birthday present, that you couldn't possibly afford without running up a huge credit card debt. What would you do?

239. If you found that your teenaged son or daughter smoked pot, how would you deal with this?

240. If your kids had no interest in sports or extracurricular activities, would you be okay with this?

241. If your 15-year-old daughter told you she wanted to be an actor, what would you tell her?

242. If your teenaged daughter told you she was pregnant from her boyfriend, how would you react?

243. How would you deal with a child of your own who was painfully shy?

244. If your child had a disability, such as autism or dyslexia that affected his progress at school and you were required to devote 14 hours a week to teaching him/ her or admitting your child to a special school, what would you do?

245. If you found out your daughter was having an affair with a neighbor's son, what would you do?

13

Communication

246. Can you talk to someone, listen attentively and also do some other task, like watching television?

247. Do you call back people, or reply to mail promptly? How long does it usually take?

248. Do you often interrupt people when they're talking?

249. Do you require the complete attention of someone, when you're speaking to them?

250. Do your phone conversations tend to be long, or brief and to-the-point?

251. How do you deal with people who don't agree with you?

252. How do you handle gossip about yourself?

253. How do you reach out to your friends, is it by sending mail, text messages, on the phone or in person?

254. Is it easy for you to see the other point of view?

255. Is it easy for you to talk about your feelings?

256. Is it easy for you to talk to someone you have just met?

257. Is there anything you would prefer to discuss with your friends, rather than with your partner?

258. Is there anything you've wanted to discuss with me but have been putting it off?

259. What is your email address?

14

Crime and the law

260. Do you own a gun? If yes, why do you need one?

261. Do you think prostitution should be legalized?

262. Have you ever been a victim of stalking or threats? Has anyone ever stalked you online?

263. Have you ever been arrested?

264. Have you ever been blackmailed? How did you deal with it?

265. Have you ever been conned?

266. Have you ever been in trouble with the law?

267. Have you ever broken any laws to get something done?

268. Have you ever broken the law?

269. Have you ever fallen for an internet scam?

270. Have you ever sued someone, or been sued? What was it all about?

271. Is there anything that you're doing right now, that you wouldn't want people to find out? Why would you want to hide it?

272. Under what circumstances do you think it would be ok to steal?

273. When do you think it is okay to break the law?

15

Current Issues

274. Are you a feminist?

275. Do you think feminism has worked for women?

276. Do you think it is okay to abort a child?

277. How important do you think it is to preserve the environment?

278. Should marijuana be legalized?

279. What are your views on capital punishment? Do you think capital punishment should be more or less frequently awarded?

280. What do you think of celebrities who endorse the fight against global warming and then charter flights to travel or drive cars with poor fuel efficiency?

281. What do you think of people who keep guns? Are you in favor of or against gun control?

282. What do you think of some actors and filmmakers who glamorize crime and terrorism through their films?

283. What do you think of vegetarianism?

284. Where do you think the country is heading?

285. Would you support a move to ban capital punishment?

16

Dating

286. After attaining adulthood, have you ever stopped dating someone because your parents didn't approve?

287. At what age did you start dating?

288. At what point do you introduce a date to your parents?

289. Did you get any dating advice from your parents, in your growing up years?

290. Have you ever answered a personal ad? Tell me about it.

291. Have you ever dated a co-worker?

292. Have you ever dated anyone you knew from work?

293. Have you ever dated someone much richer or poorer than yourself?

294. Have you ever dated someone of a different race?

295. Have you ever not kissed a date, because he or she had bad breath?

296. Have you ever placed a personals ad? How did you describe yourself? What was the experience like?

297. Have you generally dated people your own age or significantly older/younger?

298. Have you usually dated people similar to you or different?

299. How do you evaluate the people you date?

300. How do you figure out if someone is interested in you?

301. How do you show someone that you're interested in them?

302. How long do you wait before calling someone after a date? How soon do you expect to be called?

303. If someone you were dating told you they were on psychotherapy, how would you react?

304. If you were single, how would you go about meeting prospective partners?

305. To what extent is the opinion of your friends important to you, when you're dating someone?

306. What do you think your dating partners find attractive about you?

307. What type of people do you attract?

308. What's the most number of dating partners you've had, at any point of time?

309. When you think of all the people you've dated so far, have there been any common traits in them?

310. Which has been your worst date ever?

311. Which is the best pick-up line that you've heard so far? Did it work?

312. Who was your first date?

17

Death and Dying

313. Are you in favor of euthanasia for the terminally ill who have no desire to live?

314. Are you scared of death?

315. Have you ever had a near-death experience?

316. Have you written a will?

317. How long do you expect to live?

318. How old do you want to live to be?

319. How would you prefer to die?

320. If you died today and people were asked to talk about you, what would they say?

321. If you died today, how many people would attend your funeral?

322. If you had only a day to live, how would you spend it?

323. If you had only a week to live, how would you spend it?

324. If you knew you would die in 24 hours' time, what would be your biggest regret?

325. If you were to outlive your entire immediate family and had amassed a huge fortune, how would you distribute it in your will?

326. What do you think happens to us after we die?

327. What do you think of clinics in Switzerland that offer assisted suicide to those desiring to end their lives?

328. What would you like written, on your gravestone?

329. Where have we come from and where do we go after we die, according to you?

330. Which music or song would you like to be played at your funeral?

331. Would you consider donating your body or eyes after your demise?

18

Eating and Drinking

332. Are there any foods that you just don't like?

333. Are you a vegetarian?

334. Are you adventurous with food or do you generally prefer tried-and-tested fare that you're sure you like?

335. Are you okay with eating leftovers at home?

336. Can you cook?

337. Describe the perfect meal for you. How many courses would it have?

338. Do you eat everything on your plate?

339. Do you like chocolate? What sort of chocolate are you into?

340. Do you like eating junk food?

341. Do you like spicy food or sweet?

342. Do you prefer coffee or tea or neither?

343. Do you prefer coffee, tea or beer?

344. Have you ever been too drunk to know what's happening around you?

345. Have you ever played drinking games with your buddies?

346. Have you ever said or done anything after drinking, that you wish you hadn't?

347. Have you ever tried a cocktail you've really loved?

348. Have you ever tried eating any exotic animal dish?

349. How many times a week do you drink?

350. How often do you like to eat out?

351. Is there a pub that you are a regular at?

352. What do you like eating between meals?

353. What do you like having for breakfast?

354. What is the most amount of liquor you've ever consumed in an evening?

355. What sort of cuisine do you like?

356. What sort of food do you like?

357. Which flavor of ice cream do you like?

358. Which is the one food you can't imagine life without?

19

Education

359. Did you ever have to repeat a year in school or college?

360. Did you go to college? Where did you study?

361. How important do you a think a college degree is for career success?

362. How important do you think formal education is?

363. There are millions of people with graduate degrees, who're often jobless and many entrepreneurs with little formal education, who're very rich. What do you think of this?

364. If you could take two years off your work and pursue an educational course, what would it be?

365. If you had to teach anything to a group of five people, over two weeks, what would you teach?

366. What is your educational background?

367. Would you have wanted to study further than you did?

20

Entertainment

368. Are there any shows on television that you never miss?

369. Did you ever consider a career in show business?

370. Do you gamble?

371. Do you have a computer or a television in your bedroom?

372. Do you think it comes in the way of relaxing?

373. Do you like dancing?

374. Do you like watching cartoon films?

375. Do you like watching the opera?

376. How much television do you watch?

377. Is there any character from 'Friends' or 'Desperate Housewives', that you think you are like?

378. What do you like doing for fun and entertainment?

379. When your team loses in a sporting event, does it ruin your day? How long does it take for you to get over it?

380. Which clubs do you belong to? How much time do you spend there?

381. Which television series do you love watching – even reruns of?

21

Everyday life

382. Are there any activities you consider a waste of time?

383. Are you sloppy around your home?

384. Do you plan your day or take it as it comes?

385. Do you spend time on the internet?

386. Do you take a lot of time to get dressed, when you have to go out?

387. Do you use foul language or swear words often? How do you react when others do?

388. How do you deal with junk mail?

389. How do you get news? Is it through TV, newspapers or on the internet?

390. How do you handle stress?

391. How does your behavior with others change, when you are stressed?

392. How good are you with time management?

393. How long does it take for you to get dressed in the morning?

394. How long does it take you to start your day?

395. Is it easy or difficult for you to take decisions?

396. Is there anything you just have to do every day?

397. What do you do when you're bored?

398. What do you like or dislike about the city/town which you live in?

399. What do you like to wear?

400. What does your phone bill run into, usually?

401. What is a regular working day like, in your life?

402. What is the one thing you would never leave home without?

403. What motivates you to get out of bed every morning?

404. What time do you start your day?

405. When do you get bored?

406. Which are the websites you usually visit?

22

Family

407. Among your siblings, whom do you get along with the most?

408. Are your grandparents alive?

409. Did you ever have a major conflict with either of your parents?

410. Do you have any family heirlooms that are passed on to every generation?

411. Do you have siblings? If you don't, do you wish you did? If you do, do you wish you were the only child?

412. Do you like your family name? Would you ever want to change it?

413. Do you love either parent more than the other?

414. Do you think you have a healthy family?

415. Do you think you have had any inherent disadvantages because of the family you were born in, the place where you lived, your religion, race or

any other aspect of your life, that you had little or no control over?

416. Do you think your folks did a good job of raising you? Is there anything they should have done differently?

417. Do your relatives come over to stay at your place when they're in the city? Are you okay with that?

418. Have you ever given a loan to, or taken a loan from, a relative? Was it repaid back promptly?

419. Have you ever gone into a business with a relative?

420. Have you ever had a major fight with your own family?

421. Have you tried to trace your family tree?

422. How does your family celebrate Christmas?

423. How important is the opinion of your family to you?

424. How important is your family to you?

425. How much time do you spend with the family?

426. How often do you call up your dad or mom?

427. If you could change one thing about your family, what would it be?

428. If your family didn't like someone you were dating, would you stop seeing the person?

429. If your family didn't like the person you chose to marry, would you drop the person?

430. Is it easy for you to turn down your parents, when they ask you to do something that you'd rather not do?

431. Is there anyone from your family or extended family whom you no longer are on speaking terms with? What went wrong?

432. Is there anyone in your family, who doesn't approve of our getting married?

433. Is there anyone in your family you would be embarrassed to have me meet?

434. Is your family proud of you? Why?

435. Tell me about your family traditions.

436. Tell me about your family.

437. What has been the biggest fight within your family?

438. What have you learnt from your father?

439. What was your relationship with your siblings like, in your growing up years?

440. When you're out with your friends, where do you usually go? What do you do?

441. Where are you from?

442. Who are you closest to, in your family?

443. Who are you more like – your mother or father? In looks? In temperament?

23

Fantasy

444. If you could be invisible for a day, how would you spend the day?

445. If you could change one thing about your current situation, what would it be?

446. If you could give one person the elixir of youth, (not to yourself) who would that be?

447. If you could have any one superpower, what would that be?

448. If you could have been born during any era, which would you choose, a few centuries in the past or sometime in the future?

449. If you could marry any celebrity, who would it be?

450. If you could meet any one celebrity over lunch, who would it be? Why?

451. If you could solve any one problem plaguing the world, which one would it be?

452.If you could use time travel to visit a point in the past, which would that be? What if you could travel to the future?

453.If you had the choice to have been born in some other country, where would that be?

454.If you had to try and create a new Guiness record, which one would you choose?

455.If you were granted three wishes, what would they be?

456.If you were to be stranded on an island, who would you want to have for company?

457.What do you think you were, in your previous birth?

458.What would your dream home be like?

24

Favorite

459. Which is your favorite dance?

460. Are there any favorite pick-up lines or ice-breakers that you use with the opposite sex?

461. Do you have a favorite coffee shop?

462. Is there a favorite sexual position you have? What makes it your favorite?

463. Which are your favorite board games?

464. Which are your favorite television channels?

465. Which has been your favorite job, so far?

466. Which is your favorite animal?

467. Which is your favorite bird?

468. Which is your favorite book?

469. Which is your favorite car?

470. Which is your favorite cartoon character?

471. Which is your favorite color?

472. Which is your favorite corner in your home?

473. Which is your favorite corner in your house?

474. Which is your favorite day of the week?

475. Which is your favorite dessert?

476. Which is your favorite flower?

477. Which is your favorite fruit?

478. Which is your favorite gadget?

479. Which is your favorite historical figure?

480. Which is your favorite holiday?

481. Which is your favorite hour of the day?

482. Which is your favorite midnight snack?

483. Which is your favorite movie?

484. Which is your favorite music band?

485. Which is your favorite outfit?

486. Which is your favorite perfume?

487. Which is your favorite quote?

488. Which is your favorite radio station?

489. Which is your favorite restaurant?

490. Which is your favorite romantic song?

491. Which is your favorite snack?

492. Which is your favorite song?

493. Which is your favorite vegetable?

494. Which was your favorite toy, when you were a kid?

495. Who is you favorite actor?

496. Who is your favorite author?

497. Who is your favorite sportsperson?

498. Is there anything you find very irresistible?
     Chocolate, for example?

25

Fears

499. Are you afraid of growing older?

500. Are you afraid of the dark?

501. Do you believe in ghosts and spirits?

502. Is there any fear that you're trying to overcome?

503. What are you afraid of, the most?

504. Would you spend a night in a haunted house for $100,000?

26

Friends

505. Are most of your friends single or committed?

506. Are you friendly with your neighbors?

507. Are you okay with your friends dropping in at home/work without calling beforehand?

508. Are you similar to your friends, in temperament?

509. Do you consider yourself a good or a bad influence on your friends?

510. Do you have a lot of friends?

511. Do you have enough of friends? Would you rather have more or fewer friends?

512. Do you have more male or female friends?

513. Do you think you will be able to spend as much time as you do now with your friends, after you're married?

514. Do you think you would still be able to stay in touch with your friends after you're married?

515. Do your friends come to you for advice?

516. Do your friends use you as a shoulder to cry on?

517. Have you ever done anything due to peer pressure that you wouldn't have otherwise?

518. How do close friends see you?

519. How do you handle friendships when you realise you've outgrown them?

520. How do you think your friends from school would react to your persona of today?

521. How important are friendships to you?

522. How important is the opinion of your friends to you?

523. How important is the opinion of your relatives to you?

524. Is there any friend of yours that you look up to, or try to emulate?

525. Is there anything about you, that you would never want your friends to find out?

526. What do most of your friends have in common?

527. What have you learned from your friends?

528. When your friends tell you about trouble they're having with their partners, are you able to see things from the other's point of view too?

529. Which is your oldest friendship? Why do you think it has lasted so long?

530. Who are the people you know that you would trust with your life?

531. Who is your 3 am friend, someone you could call anytime and he/she would rush to your help?

532. Who is your closest friend?

533. Who is your most successful friend? Do you ever feel envious or jealous of your friend?

27

Gambling

534. Do you bet on horses? What is the largest amount you have ever won or lost, betting on horses?

535. Do you bet on sporting events?

536. Do you play poker?

28

Games

537. Do you like role-playing games?

538. Do you play any video games or any MMORPGs (Massively multiplayer online role playing games)?

539. Do you play bingo? Are you lucky with it?

540. Have you ever played Truth or Dare? What was it like?

541. Which are the card games you like?

29

Getting Married

542. Are you mentally, emotionally and financially ready to get married?

543. Do you feel the pressure to get married?

544. Have you ever been under pressure to marry a specific person?

545. Have you ever felt insecure about finding the right partner and getting married?

546. Have you ever turned down someone who wanted to marry you, and later regretted doing so?

547. How do you think getting married would change your relationship with your partner?

548. How long do you think a couple should stay engaged before they marry?

549. How much money would make you feel secure and ready to get married?

550. If you were marrying someone much wealthier than yourself and were asked to sign a prenuptial

agreement, would you do it? Would the suggestion offend you?

551. What are you looking for in a spouse?

552. What are your needs and expectations from a marriage?

553. What do you tell people when they ask you why you haven't married yet?

554. When do you expect to get married?

555. When you get married, would you share the wedding expenses with your partner or would you expect them to foot the entire bill?

556. Why do you think so many single people are anxious to get married, even while so many married couples head for divorces?

557. Would you consider marrying someone of a different nationality or faith?

558. Would you delay getting married until you are financially more secure?

559. Would you like to get married in some unusual manner, like underwater or in an airplane?

560. Would you like to get married someday? If no, why not?

561. Would you marry someone, years older to you, if he was a multimillionaire?

562. Would you marry someone, if you knew your parents didn't approve of them?

563. Would you marry someone who was far superior to you in some way - intellectually, in wealth or in looks?

564. Would you marry someone who was significantly more or less educated than you?

565. Would you marry someone you didn't find particularly attractive, but who was very wealthy?

566. Would you marry someone you didn't have any chemistry with but who was very good natured?

567. Would you prefer that your spouse works, or would you rather he or she stayed at home to look after the kids?

568. Would you rather be single than have a bad marriage, or is 'something' better than 'nothing' for you?

569. Would you rather marry someone richer or poorer than you?

30

Health

570. Are you able to do physically strenuous work?

571. Are you very health conscious?

572. Do you exercise?

573. Do you feel healthy?

574. Do you go for a health checkup every year?

575. Do you have any allergies?

576. Do you have health insurance?

577. Do you think you need any kind of therapy? What kind? How would it help you?

578. Do you think you're in good shape for your age?

579. Have you ever been hospitalized? What was it like?

580. Have you ever been in a serious accident?

581. Have you ever been tested for STD or HIV? What was the result?

582. Have you ever had counseling?

583. Have you ever had psychological problems or visited a psychologist?

584. Have you ever had to get any surgery done?

585. Have you ever tried to lose weight?

586. How do you deal with PMS?

587. How does PMS affect your moods?

588. How likely are you to take medicines, if you have a minor ailment?

589. How long do your periods and PMS (Premenstrual Syndrome) last?

590. How often do you fall sick?

591. When you have a dental problem, do you put off going to the dentist?

592. Would you rather be fatter or thinner than you currently are?

31

Highs and Lows

593. What are you most grateful for?

594. What's the nicest thing someone's ever done for you?

595. Which has been the best day of your life, so far? Describe it.

596. Which has been the most hilarious prank you've ever played on someone?

597. Which have been the happiest moments of your life?

598. Which have been the turning points in your life?

599. Which is the dumbest thing you have ever done?

600. Which is the most memorable gift you have ever received?

601. Who is the biggest celebrity you have ever met?

602. Has anyone you trusted ever let you down?

32

History

603. If you could have anyone from history, as a dinner guest, who would it be?

604. What do you think of people who admire Adolf Hitler?

605. Which is the most useful invention of all time, according to you?

606. Which scientific discovery do you think was the most important ever?

33

Hobbies

607. Are there any specific hobbies you have?

608. Do you like to dance?

609. Is there anything you collect?

34

Holidays

610. How much do you spend on Christmas?

611. How much time do you spend, thinking up Christmas gifts?

612. If you could spend a day on a picnic, how would you plan it?

613. If you didn't receive any gifts for Christmas, or got gifts you weren't happy with, how would you react?

614. Which are the Christmas gifts you remember getting, as a child?

615. Whom do you buy gifts for during Christmas?

35

Infidelity

616. Do you think men, by nature, are polygamous?

617. Have you ever cheated on a partner?

618. Have you ever felt tempted to have an extramarital affair? How did you deal with it?

619. Have you ever had an affair with someone, who was cheating on their partner?

620. How important do you think monogamy is? How far is it possible to remain monogamous?

621. If your spouse confessed to having had a brief fling, how would you react?

622. If your wife told you that you weren't the father of your ten year old child whom you had lovingly raised, how would you react?

623. Is it easy for you to trust your lover?

624. What do you think is the motivation for adultery?

625. What do you think of polyandry?

626. What do you think of polygamy as a practice?

627. What is the longest period of time that you have been monogamous?

628. What percentage of married men, do you think cheat on their wives?

629. What would you do if you found out I was cheating on you?

630. Why do you think people cheat on their partners?

631. Would you ever consider having an affair with someone who was married? What if the person was going through a bad marriage?

36

Inner self

632. Are you able to truly forgive and forget?

633. Are your decisions ruled more by your heart or your head?

634. Do you keep a diary?

635. Do you keep secrets from your family?

636. Do you think you have intuitive ability?

637. How much are you in touch with your inner feelings?

638. How often do you follow your gut feeling? Does it usually work for you?

639. What gives you a feeling of safety and security?

640. What makes you laugh?

641. What sort of dreams do you see?

642. What would make you very happy?

643. Which is the worst aspect of your personality? What brings it out?

37

Interests

644. Do you enjoy arguing and debating?

645. Do you like solving puzzles?

646. How many books do you read in a year? Which are your favorite subjects?

647. How often do you visit bookshops?

38

Let's talk about me!

648. If I was unemployed for a long stretch of time, would your approach towards me change?

649. Do you think I have a sense of humor?

650. Do you feel the need to be very patient with me?

651. Do you sometimes know what I'm about to say, before I even say it?

652. Do you think I have good dress sense? Do you like the way I dress?

653. Do you think I nag you?

654. Do you think I should take life more seriously, or less seriously than I do?

655. Do you think I try to change you?

656. How easy or difficult is it for you to gauge my mood, from my body language?

657. If we were chatting on the internet and you wanted to confirm my identity, which is the one question you would ask me?

658. If you could change one thing about me, what would it be?

659. In which ways do you think we are similar or different?

660. Is there any aspect of my personality that makes you proud?

661. Is there anything I can do to make myself more attractive?

662. Is there anything I do that makes you feel uncomfortable?

663. Of all the gifts you have ever received from me, which one do you treasure the most?

664. Tell me five things you don't like about me.

665. Tell me five things you like about me.

666. What did you first find attractive about me, when we met? Do you still find it as attractive?

667. What do you find most attractive about me?

668. What was your first impression of me?

669. Which of my outfits do you hate?

670. Which outfits of mine do you like the most?

39

Life

671. Are you satisfied with the way you live your life?

672. Do you look forward to the future?

673. Do you think life is unfair?

674. Do you worry about growing old?

675. Has any book changed your perception of life?

676. Has there been any incident that changed the way you looked at life?

677. Have you ever lived alone for any period of time?

678. How far ahead in life do you like to plan for?

679. How has age affected you? Are there things you could do ten years back, but can't now?

680. If I asked you, which have been the most memorable days of your life so far, which would they be?

681. If you could swap your life with that of anyone else, who would it be?

682. If you lost everything and had to start life anew, how do you think you would cope with it and how successful do you think you would be, in rebuilding everything that you now have?

683. In which aspects of your life are you very secure?

684. Is there any area of your life where you are very insecure, at this point?

685. Is there any country you would like to migrate to? What stops you from doing so?

686. What are you looking forward to, at this point of time?

687. What has been the biggest disappointment so far?

688. What has been your biggest personal challenge to date?

689. What makes life worth living?

690. Which are the lessons that life has taught you so far?

691. Which has been the happiest phase of your life so far?

692. Which has been your most embarrassing moment?

693. Who are the people in your life, you would do anything for?

694. Who is your role model?

695. Whom do you admire the most?

40

Love

696. Do you believe all is fair in love and war?

697. Do you believe in love at first sight?

698. Do you believe in true love?

699. Do you believe that in relationships, one person loves and the other person lets themselves be loved?

700. Do you mentally compare your lover to lovers from the past?

701. Do you continue to stay in touch with your exes?

702. Do you prefer loving or being loved?

703. Do you really believe that love means never having to say you're sorry?

704. Do you think 'falling in love' is usually a delusion?

705. Do you think it is okay to date more than one person at one time? When do you think one should move to exclusively seeing a single person?

706. Do you think living together for some period of time is a good idea, if you plan to get married?

707. Do you think people tend to be on their best behavior when dating?

708. Do you think that over a period of time, one can fall in love with someone who one lives with?

709. Have you always fallen in love with a similar personality type?

710. Have you ever aborted a child or asked a lover to abort one?

711. Have you ever been in love with someone and not told them about it?

712. Have you ever been in love with two people at the same time?

713. Have you ever been loved unconditionally?

714. Have you ever conveyed that you love someone more than you really did? Why did you do this?

715. Have you ever fallen in love with someone, knowing that they were just not the sort of person you would want to marry?

716. Have you ever had your heart broken by someone you loved?

717. Have you ever known someone you thought was a soul mate?

718.Have you ever lost a loved one? How did you deal with it?

719.Have you ever loved someone so intensely as to be willing to lay down your life for them?

720.Have you ever loved someone you had very little respect for?

721.Have you ever schemed, manipulated or played games to win someone's love and affection?

722.Have you saved old love notes and memorabilia from several years ago?

723.How do you know when you're in love?

724.How has your definition of love changed over the years? What was it like before and what is it now?

725.How many people have you been in love with, so far?

726.How many people have you confessed your love to, over the years?

727.If someone you were in love with, turned you down, how would you deal with it?

728.If you were invited to a couples-only event, who would you take along with you?

729.Is it easy for you to cope with rejection?

730.Is it easy for you to fall in love?

731.Is there anyone you've been in love with, whom you still care for?

732. So far how many people have confessed their love for you?

733. What are the various ways in which you would want your partner to show his/her love for you?

734. What are you like, when you fall in love?

735. What do you like most about being single?

736. What does love mean to you?

737. What has been your worst experience with a lover?

738. What is the longest you've gone between relationships?

739. Did you enjoy being single, or if you're single now, are you looking forward to getting hitched again?

740. What do you hate about being single and what do you love about it?

741. When did you first realize you had fallen in love with me?

742. Who was your first love?

41

Loyalties

743. Is there any person you cannot turn down a request from?

744. Is there anyone you can give up your life for?

745. Is there anyone you can never say no to?

42

Managing the house

746. Can you replace your car tyre all by yourself?

747. Do you clean the bathroom yourself?

748. Do you do the dishes after every meal, or is it once in a day?

749. Do you have pests in your home? Have you ever contacted a professional company to deal with them?

750. Do you have plants at home? Who looks after them?

751. Do you keep things that you may never need again - very old bills, brochures, magazines etc? If your partner thought that a lot of this was junk and should be thrown out, would you do that?

752. Do you plan in advance the chores which you have to do or do them when you feel like?

753. Have you ever painted your house yourself?

754. How clean do you ensure your house is?

755. How many hours every week do you spend looking after your house?

756. How often do you change the sheets?

757. How warm do you like your house to be during winter?

758. If you could do up your house the way you wanted to, which style would you opt for?

759. What are your expectations from a home?

760. What sort of furniture would you like for your home - contemporary, antique, ethnic?

761. Who does the laundry at home?

762. Would you like to grow fruits and vegetables in a garden?

763. Would you like to have a front lawn?

764. Would you want to have an apartment, condominium or a stand alone house? Do you consider the amount of work involved in maintaining such a house?

43

Marriage

765. Are there certain home responsibilities that you wouldn't want to take up, after you're married?

766. At what point do you think a couple would know each other enough to consider marrying each other?

767. Do you believe that a lot of effort goes into making a marriage work?

768. Do you believe that your marriage will be successful?

769. Do you think a person should keep his or her partner informed about where they are going to be at any given time?

770. Do you think it is okay to correct your partner in the presence of others?

771. Do you think that traditional roles within a marriage, for the man and woman, work better?

772. Have you ever been married?

773. How do you think a couple should celebrate a wedding anniversary?

774. How long do you think a couple should give to their marriage, to make it work, before giving up and deciding to part ways?

775. How long do you think a couple should try to make a marriage work, before opting for a divorce?

776. How soon after getting married, would you want to start a family?

777. If you died, how long would you want your spouse to wait before dating or remarrying, if at all?

778. If you were married and a family friend at a party made a pass at you, how would you handle it?

779. If your partner had kids from an earlier marriage and wanted to stay in touch with them, would it be acceptable to you?

780. If your spouse died, how long would you wait before dating or getting married again?

781. If your spouse got addicted to alcohol and it was affecting his/her work, what would you do?

782. If your spouse had to work in a different country for a couple of years and could only visit you once every few months, do you think you could still stay loyal?

783. If your spouse slapped you in the heat of an argument, what would you do?

784. If your spouse wanted to pursue ambitions that would take long to attain and required your financial support until then, would you cooperate?

785. What can be the one reason for you to immediately walk out of a marriage?

786. What could be the reason for you to divorce someone you were married to?

787. What do you feel about couples who have been married together for 25 years, or even 50 years?

788. What do you think about couples who renew their vows after staying married for 25 years?

789. What do you think of arranged marriages in countries like India, where couples sometimes barely know each other when they marry?

790. What if you were married or also had kids, and you found that your spouse was cheating on you?

791. When we marry, would we pool together all our resources or would we keep our monies separate?

792. When we have a baby would you share the responsibilities of attending to it?

793. When you get married, would you like it to be a quiet affair or one where you call everyone you know?

794. Which are the valid reasons for a divorce, according to you?

795. Which aspect of our marriage are you most satisfied with? Which aspect are you dissatisfied with?

796. Which is the advice that you wish someone had given you before you got married?

797. Why do you think most marriages in the United States end in divorces?

798. Would you be okay with your spouse going on a vacation alone, without you?

799. Would you want to have an equation with your spouse, that is similar to the equation your parents shared?

800. Would you want your wife to change her last name? What if she wanted to retain her own last name?

44

Miscellaneous

801. Are there any places that you're particularly sentimental about?

802. Are there any possessions you're very sentimental about?

803. Are there any subjects that you are not comfortable discussing? What makes you uncomfortable about them?

804. Are you more likely to support a favorite or the under-dog?

805. Are you usually able to keep your new year resolutions? If no, how long does it take for you to break them?

806. Can you say this tongue twister fast - "She sells sea-shells on the sea shore, but the sea-shells that she sells on the sea shore are not the sea shells we find on the sea shore"?

807. Do you believe there is life on other planets?

808. Do you daydream?

809. Do you like your name? Have you ever considered changing it?

810. Do you prefer a warm or cold climate?

811. Have you considered making changes to your name to bring luck, as per numerology or kabbalah?

812. How do you find sick and gross jokes?

813. How do you generally react, when someone asks you for a favor?

814. If you had to do without one of the five senses, which one would it be?

815. If your house was on fire, but if you hurried, you could save any three articles, what would you save?

816. Were you named after someone?

817. What does it take for you to trust people?

818. What is the nicest thing you have ever done for someone?

819. When was the last time you went really out of your way for someone?

820. When was the last time you were overwhelmed by something that someone did for you?

821. When you need an honest opinion about something, who do you go to for it? What makes you trust this person?

822. When you need to talk to someone, who do you turn to?

823. Which are the subjects on which you think you're qualified to counsel others, or offer advice?

824. Which is your biggest challenge at this point of time?

45

Money

825. Are you a spendthrift or are you thrifty?

826. Are your expenses less than your income currently?

827. Are you satisfied with your financial progress so far?

828. Do you believe everyone must have life insurance? How much are you insured for?

829. Do you have any financial goals for the next five or ten years? What are they?

830. Do you have financial acumen?

831. Do you have to keep up with the Joneses?

832. Do you invest in stocks?

833. Do you often buy luxury items you have no use for?

834. Do you often buy things that you don't need?

835. Do you think I can be trusted with money?

836. Do you think you are obsessed with money and material possessions?

837. Do you think you understand the value of money?

838. Do you think you're adept at managing money?

839. Do you usually pay off the outstanding balance on your credit card, or do you carry it forward?

840. Do you usually save money to buy big-ticket items or do you fund them with loans and credit card debt?

841. Have you drawn a will? Why not?

842. Have you ever been flat broke? How did you deal with it?

843. Have you ever been to a debt counsellor?

844. Have you ever declared bankruptcy?

845. Have you ever evaded taxes?

846. Have you ever felt that someone used you for money?

847. Have you ever had a garage sale?

848. Have you ever loaned someone a lot of money and not got it back?

849. Have you ever made money from investing in real estate?

850. Have you ever managed two or more jobs?

851. Have you ever won a lottery?

852. How did you make your first dollar?

853. How do you manage expenses and the monthly budget?

854. How frequently do you check your bank account?

855. How good are you at managing money?

856. How important is it that your partner understands the value of money?

857. How important is money to you?

858. How many credit cards do you have?

859. How much debt have you taken on?

860. How much do you owe on your credit cards now?

861. How much do you spend on cigarettes and booze every month?

862. How much do you tip at restaurants?

863. How much money do you spend every month?

864. How much of a 'financial buffer' would you want to have, to guard against a rough patch?

865. How much time and money do you spend every week, on looking good?

866. How rich do you want to be?

867. How would you prepare for a financial emergency?

868. How would you react if your spouse started making substantially more money than you?

869. If money were not a consideration, which profession would you want to pursue?

870. If we had to cut costs and lower our standard of living, would you be able to do it?

871. If you found, that your partner had been stashing away money in a bank account without your knowledge, how would you react?

872. If you inherited a million dollars what would you do with it?

873. If you started making much more money than you currently make, what changes would you make to your current lifestyle?

874. If you started making twice as much as you make now, what are the changes you would bring about in your lifestyle?

875. If you were asked to give away $1 million in charity, which organizations or people will the money go to?

876. If you were given a million dollars to change to some other faith – let's say, convert to Islam, would you do that? If you're a Muslim and were asked to convert to Christianity?

877. If you were given a million dollars to invest all of it, where would you put it?

878.If you were in a financial mess, how would you plan to come out of it?

879.If you won or inherited a billion dollars, what would you do with the money?

880.If your income reduced and you had to cut costs, where would you do so?

881.Is money often a source of worry for you?

882.Is time more important to you than money? Do you sometimes pay more to get something done quicker?

883.What did you do with the money you won?

884.What do you think of someone like Warren Buffet giving away most of his fortune to charity? Would you ever consider doing it?

885.What is the most you would spend on a bottle of wine?

886.What is your credit like - good, bad or poor?

887.Which is your biggest monthly expense?

888.Who takes care of your accounting and taxes?

889.With how much money would you feel financially stable?

890.Would you change over to a completely different career if you knew it would bring you more money?

891.Would you consider posing nude for 'Playboy' magazine for a million dollars? Would you do it for a cause you believed in, even if you weren't benefiting financially?

892. Would you keep your money in a joint account with your partner, or would you rather keep the accounts separate?

893. Would you prefer to have a debt-free and frugal wedding or one which is lavish, but which would saddle you with a debt of thousands of dollars?

894. Would you rather be extremely rich, good-looking and successful and die in the next five years, or be moderately successful and live to be 90?

895. Would you want to have a pre-nuptial agreement before you marry?

46

Morals and Ethics

896. Do you believe that everything in life is for sale, waiting for the right price to be offered?

897. Do you think a person should give a percentage of his earnings to charity? How much is a fair percentage?

898. Have you ever bribed a government servant?

899. Have you ever cheated in an exam? Were you caught?

900. Have you ever stolen anything? Were you caught?

901. How ethical are you, when it comes to getting your way?

902. If an unborn child was diagnosed with a serious illness, would you favor terminating the pregnancy?

903. If you found out that you were pregnant but weren't yet married, how would you deal with it?

904. If your country was at war, would you enlist in the army?

905. What do you think of censorship in cinema? Do you think it must be stricter or should it give way to self-censorship?

906. What is the cruelest thing you've ever done?

907. When would it be okay to lie, according to you?

908. Which is the biggest lie you've ever told?

909. Would you get pregnant without your husband's consent, if he wanted to delay starting a family?

47

Movies

910. Do you like watching horror films? Do you scare easily?

911. How many movies do you watch every month? Which genre is your favorite?

912. What sort of movies do you watch?

913. When you watch a movie, which row and seat do you like to sit in?

914. Which is the first movie you ever saw?

915. Which is the worst movie you've ever seen?

916. Which was the last movie you saw?

48

Parents

917.As a child, how did you perceive your mother?

918.Did either of your parents cheat on the other?

919.Did you ever find one of your parents lying to or keeping secrets from the other?

920.Did your parents ever compare you to your siblings during your growing up years? How did you deal with this?

921.Did your parents play traditional stereotypical roles within their marriage?

922.Did your parents spend most of their time together, or away from each other?

923.Do you resent either or both of your parents for breaking their marriage?

924.Do you think you would have been happier living with the parent you stayed away from?

925.Has your parents' marriage conditioned the way you approach relationships?

926.How did your parents discipline you, in your childhood?

927.How did your parents treat each other?

928. How do you think they have been able to make a success of their marriage?

929. If I had a major conflict with your mother or father and you had to support one side, which one would it be?

930. If their marriage didn't work out, what do you think went wrong?

931. Is there any aspect of your parent's marriage that you would want to definitely be a part of your own marriage?

932. Is there any aspect of your parent's marriage that you would never want should be a part of your own marriage?

933. Is there anything in your life that you blame your parents for?

934. What advice about the opposite sex did you receive from either parent, during your growing up years?

935. What sort of partner would your parents want for you?

936. What was it like, growing up with a single parent?

937. What was the equation like, with your parents? Who had the upper hand in their relationship?

938. What was your relationship like, with your father, during your growing up years?

939. Which factors do you think were responsible for the success of your parents' marriage?

940. Who had the final word in major decisions, within your family?

941. Would you blame either of your parents for the breakdown of their marriage?

942. Would you consider your parents' marriage to be a successful one?

943. Would you support your parents financially, when they retire?

944. Would you want to move to a place far away from where you parents live?

49

People Skills

945. Are there any subjects that bore you, in conversation?

946. Are you comfortable speaking to a large group of people? Does it matter if you know most of them, or they're strangers?

947. Do you always like to have the last word?

948. Do you believe everyone is to be trusted, till they let you down, or is no one to be trusted until they have earned the privilege?

949. Do you find it easy or difficult to hold the attention of people, when you talk to them?

950. Do you like large crowds of people?

951. Do you like people, by and large?

952. Do you think most people are dishonest?

953. Do you think you are a good listener? Do you think I am?

954. Do you think you're always right, or at least right on most occasions?

955. How do you deal with people who don't share your point of view?

956. How do you deal with rude people?

957. How often do you compliment people?

958. How often do you talk to strangers?

959. How well acquainted are you with your neighbors?

960. If I criticized you or disagreed with you in the presence of other people, how would it affect you?

961. If you're at a party where you know only the host, would you sit in a corner by yourself, go out and talk to people yourself or get the host to introduce you to someone?

962. Is it easy for you to make new friends?

963. Is it easy or difficult for you to see through people?

964. Would you be comfortable at a get-together where you didn't know anyone except the host?

965. Would you be comfortable giving a speech before a large gathering?

50

Personality

966. Are there any books or movies, that have had a major impact on your life or otherwise influenced you?

967. Are there days when you don't feel like talking to anyone and would rather be left alone?

968. When drunk, have you ever done something you regretted later?

969. Are there times when you really need a hug? Do you hug people often?

970. Are you a clean person?

971. Are you a demonstrative person?

972. Are you a morning person or a night person?

973. Are you a quiet person or a loud one?

974. Are you accident-prone?

975. Are you forgetful? Do you get offended when people close to you remind you of tasks?

976. Are you likely to make to-do lists if you have a lot of things to do on a given day?

977. Are you patient with people who are very verbose in their conversation?

978. Are you quick to decide or do you take a long time?

979. Are you usually punctual?

980. Are you very systematic and organized?

981. Do you consider yourself a leader or a follower?

982. Do you like being around people?

983. Do you think you have exhibitionistic tendencies?

984. Do you think you have voyeuristic tendencies?

985. Do you think you're a spontaneous person?

986. Do you think you're jealous? What makes you so?

987. Have you ever come close to killing yourself or harming yourself seriously?

988. Have you ever felt completely helpless?

989. How do you go about offering criticism?

990. How do you like to be pampered?

991. How do you react when you're asked to wait at a restaurant that is packed?

992. How do you relax?

993. How fashion conscious are you?

994. How many times a day do you take a bath?

995. How often do you shave?

996. How patriotic are you?

997. If I have to discuss something about you or your behaviour that I don't like, how can I bring it up without offending you?

998. If you could be an authority on any subject, what would it be?

999. If you could change any one aspect of your personality, what would it be?

1000. If you could do up your home in any way you desired and money was not a constraint, how would you do it up?

1001. If you're in a foul mood, how should others react to it?

1002. In the face of conflict, how likely are you to compromise?

1003. In which areas of life are you completely self-reliant?

1004. Is it easy for you to move with the changing times?

1005. Is there anyone who knows everything about you?

1006. Is there anything you hate doing and keep procrastinating about?

1007. Lead, follow, or get out of the way. What are you most likely to do?

1008. What is your greatest worry, currently?

1009. What makes you nostalgic?

1010. What turns you off?

1011. What turns you on?

1012. Which are the areas where you find yourself helpless?

1013. Which is the most selfish thing you've ever done?

1014. Which is the most selfless thing you've ever done?

1015. Which is your biggest flaw?

1016. Which season do you like the most?

1017. Which task do you keep putting off?

1018. Whom do you share your innermost feelings with?

1019. Would you color your hair when it starts greying?

51

Pet Peeves

1020. Are you able to put up with people who are sloppy eaters, or those who have poor table manners?

1021. Is there anything that you especially hate doing? Why do you do it?

1022. What are your pet peeves?

1023. Which are the tasks that irritate you?

1024. Which are the tasks you consider a waste of your time?

52

Politics

1025. Are you able to disagree with people on politics, morality and ethics and still remain cordial with them?

1026. Do you follow politics? Are you a liberal or a conservative, a leftist or a right wing supporter?

1027. Do you think the richest sections of our society should be taxed heavily, to distribute wealth more equitably?

1028. Do you think there is such a thing as an honest politician or is it an oxymoron?

1029. Do you vote in every election?

1030. Have you ever been part of a political protest or demonstration?

1031. Have you ever thought about entering politics?

1032. If you could be the president of your country, what would you want to change?

1033. If you could change anything about our education system, what would it be?

1034. If you had to join a political party, which one would it be?

1035. Is there any politician, you have high regard for?

1036. What do you think of communism?

1037. Which are the most important issues in today's political scenario, in your view?

53

Race and Ethnicity

1038. Is there any race of people which you prefer not to associate with?

1039. Do you think you're racist in your approach?

1040. Have you ever been a victim of racism?

1041. How do you see illegal immigrants? Do you think they should be rehabilitated, or just deported back to their country of origin?

1042. How do you see racist jokes?

1043. What challenges do you think a mixed race couple would encounter?

54

Recreation

1044. Do you bet on sports events?

1045. Do you ever go cycling into the countryside?

1046. Do you go fishing?

1047. Do you like gossip?

1048. Do you like the outdoors, or prefer the indoors?

1049. Do you think gambling should be legal in every country?

1050. Have you ever attended a rave party?

1051. How do you like to spend weekends?

1052. If you could take a day off and spend it as you pleased, how would you do it?

1053. What sort of reading are you into?

1054. When was the last time you went to an amusement park?

1055. When was the last time you went to the beach?

55

Relationships

1056. Are there any aspects of your life with your partner, that you wouldn't be comfortable discussing with others?

1057. Are there any habits of your partner, that completely annoy you?

1058. Would it bother you if a friend of yours started dating your ex?

1059. Are there any sacrifices you make, to keep a relationship going?

1060. Are you comfortable with your partner's past?

1061. Are you happy with the amount of time you and your partner spend together? Would you rather spend more or less time together?

1062. Are you open to making changes to your appearance, if your partner wanted you to?

1063. Are you possessive in your relationships?

1064. At a social do, would it bother you if your partner danced with someone else?

1065. Can you discuss anything with your partner, or are there subjects that require a delicate approach?

1066. Can you talk to me about anything you want to, without hesitation?

1067. Do you consider yourself superior or inferior to your partner in any way?

1068. Do you expect monogamy from your partner?

1069. Do you feel comfortable sharing your feelings with your partner?

1070. Do you foresee anything becoming a major issue between us, in the future?

1071. Do you get along with your partner's family?

1072. Do you like the pet names that your partner uses, to address you?

1073. Do you like your partner indulging in baby talk?

1074. Do you like your partner's friends? Is there anyone in particular that you don't like?

1075. Do you need to be in a relationship at any given time, to feel complete?

1076. Do you play games to manipulate your partner, when in a relationship?

1077. Do you remember how we first met?

1078. Do you think or feel that your partner gives you the respect you deserve?

1079. Do you think I take you for granted?

1080. Do you think it is healthy for a couple to argue and fight?

1081. Do you think it is okay for a person to discuss his or her relationship problems with close friends?

1082. Do you think it's possible to change aspects of your partner's personality?

1083. Do you think two people in a relationship must be completely honest with each other?

1084. Do you think we can have a successful long term relationship without much effort, or would we really have to try to make it a success?

1085. Do you think we fight fair?

1086. Do you think you get more praise, or criticism from your partner?

1087. Do you think your partner has double standards?

1088. Do you think your partner is as patient as you would like him/her to be?

1089. Do you think your partner should take greater pride in your achievements?

1090. Does your partner discuss a gamut of subjects, or does he/she have only a few favorite topics?

1091. Does your partner look after you when you're sick?

1092. Has it ever been very difficult for you to get over someone?

1093. Have all your relationships been with people who are more or less similar in their looks?

1094. Have you ended your relationships, or has the other person chosen to end them?

1095. Have you ever been dumped?

1096. Have you ever been hit by someone you were in a relationship with?

1097. Have you ever been in a clandestine relationship?

1098. Have you ever been in a live-in relationship?

1099. Have you ever been in a long distance relationship?

1100. Have you ever been part of a bad break up?

1101. Have you ever dumped someone?

1102. Have you ever felt insanely jealous?

1103. Have you ever hit anyone you were in a relationship with?

1104. Have you ever seen an abusive relationship, in which one partner continues to put up with the other, closely?

1105. Have you ever spied on someone you loved?

1106. Have your expectations from a partner changed as you have grown older?

1107. How communicative are you with a partner?

1108. How do you feel when we fight?

1109. How do you like your partner to introduce you?

1110. How do your kids from an earlier marriage perceive your partner?

1111. How have your expectations from a partner changed over the years?

1112. How important is intelligence to you, in a partner?

1113. How important is it that your parents like your partner?

1114. How important is it to you that your partner frequently compliments you?

1115. How important is it to you that your partner has a sense of humor?

1116. How much space do you need in a relationship?

1117. How much time can you give to your partner, in a single day?

1118. How much time every day, do you think, couples should spend with each other to keep the relationships stable and yet give space to each other?

1119. How would you rate the communication between you and your partner? Do you think it needs improvement?

1120. How would you react if your partner bellowed at you for something?

1121. How would you react if your partner didn't like your parents and told you about it, in so many words?

1122. How would you react if your partner was sulking?

1123. If someone you were seeing always stood you up on dates, what would you do?

1124. If we were heading for a split, what would you do to prevent it? Would you make any changes to yourself?

1125. If you and your partner were completely honest with each other about everything, how would it affect your relationship?

1126. If you and your partner were having trouble in your marriage, would you involve one or both of your parents, to help resolve it?

1127. If you came across the private diary of your partner, would you read it?

1128. If you came into a large inheritance, would you have more say in how it was to be spent or invested, than your partner?

1129. If you didn't like you partner's hair style, how would you deal with it?

1130. If you found out that your partner was on drugs, what would you do?

1131. If you found out that your partner went to a strip club over the weekend, when you were out of town, how would you react?

1132. If you found that your partner was emotionally involved with someone, but the relationship was purely platonic, how would you react? What if your partner had indulged in a one-night-stand with someone he/she wasn't attached to at all?

1133. If you found your partner flirting with someone, how would you react?

1134. If you have a problem with your in-laws would you rather talk to your partner or to them directly?

1135. If you have kids from an earlier marriage, was it easy for you to introduce your partner to them?

1136. If you were engaged to someone who confessed that they had fallen in love with someone else, how would you react?

1137. If you were seeing someone who suddenly told you that they wanted out of the relationship, how would you react?

1138. If your in-laws offend you, would you expect your partner to rise to your defense?

1139. If your parents and your partner have a major row and you had to pick a side, which one would it be?

1140. If your partner called you at work, would you be ok with that?

1141. If your partner got a new haircut which you didn't like, would you let them know?

1142. If your partner had a bachelor or bachelorette party before the wedding and you learnt that the party had a performance by a stripper, how would you react?

1143. If your partner had body odor, how would you handle it?

1144. If your partner loved a sport that you hated, how would you deal with it?

1145. If your partner put on a lot of weight, how would you deal with it?

1146. If your partner tells you that there are some aspects of their past that they would prefer not to discuss, would you be able to drop those subjects altogether?

1147. If your partner threatened to walk out if you didn't give away your pet, what would you do?

1148. If your partner told you that you had body odor, would you be offended?

1149. If your partner wanted to pursue a hobby or a professional goal and would be able to give you less time, would that be acceptable to you?

1150. If your partner wanted to take a break of a month from your relationship to gain a fresh perspective, would you be ok with it?

1151. If your partner wanted you to spend less time with your friends than you do, how would you react?

1152. If your partner was a workaholic how would you cope with it?

1153. If your partner was spending too much time with their friends and relatively less time with you, how would you deal with this?

1154. If your partner went traveling for a month, which are the inconveniences you anticipate in your daily routine?

1155. If your partner's friends or family stay overnight at your place, would you be ok with that?

1156. If your pet was aggressive with your partner, how would you deal with it?

1157. In what way do you express love differently than your partner?

1158. In what way would you change yourself for your partner?

1159. In what ways do you think men and women are different?

1160. In which areas do you think there is room for improvement, in our relationship?

1161. In your opinion, how long does it take to know a partner well?

1162. Is it important to you that your partner have the same political affiliation as your own?

1163. Is there any break up that you regret?

1164. Is there any couple that you admire and who you would want to emulate?

1165. Is there any relationship you have been in that you regret deeply?

1166. Is there anything I could do to make your life more comfortable?

1167. Is there anything that you would be more comfortable discussing with your friends than with your partner?

1168. Is there anything you wouldn't want your partner to wear?

1169. Is there anything you've always wanted to ask me but have been afraid to?

1170. Is there some aspect of your partner's persona that you would like to imbibe in your own?

1171. Is your partner as moral and honest as you would like them to be?

1172. What about your partner's personality do you admire the most?

1173. What did or didn't you like about your earlier partners?

1174. What do you look for in a relationship?

1175. What do you remember of our courtship?

1176. What do you think of relationships where the man is twenty or more years older than the woman? What if the woman was that much older than the man?

1177. What do you think of the irony of permanent tattoos in an age where our most relationships don't survive long?

1178. What does your partner do that makes you feel loved and desired?

1179. What is most important for you in a relationship?

1180. What is the best piece of advice you've got about relationships? Whom did you get it from?

1181. What is the longest that any of your relationships have lasted?

1182. What is the most unforgivable thing that a partner has done to you?

1183. What is your biggest fear about committing to a relationship?

1184. What is your fondest memory of all the years we have spent together?

1185. What would be more important to you than your partner?

1186. What would make you lose respect for your partner?

1187. What would you consider a truly satisfying relationship?

1188. What would you do if you found your partner had been cheating on you?

1189. When you have differences with your partner, do you discuss them with family or friends?

1190. Which are the qualities that your partner must have - not having them would be a deal breaker?

1191. Which are your partner's weaknesses?

1192. Which aspect of our life together would you want to wish away?

1193. Which has been your longest relationship and what went wrong eventually?

1194. Why have your relationships ended?

1195. Would it be okay if your partner read your mail? What about emails and text messages on your cell phone?

1196. Would you ask your partner, before inviting your friends over for dinner?

1197. Would you be comfortable interacting with former lovers of your partner?

1198. Would you be open to your partner making changes in your personality?

1199. Would you change your hairstyle for your partner?

1200. Would you have an extramarital affair, if there was virtually no possibility of your partner finding out?

1201. Would you lend money to an ex?

1202. Would you lose weight if your partner thought you were too fat?

1203. Would you want to spend more or less time with your partner than you currently do?

56

Relatives

1204. Are there any particular relatives you don't like?

1205. Is there any relative who you're especially fond of?

1206. Tell me about your relatives.

57

Religion

1207. Are there any religious beliefs that you do not have conviction in?

1208. Are you a spiritual person?

1209. Are you afraid of God?

1210. Are you an active member of your local parish?

1211. Do you attend religious services alone, or with your partner?

1212. Do you believe God is male or female or androgynous?

1213. Do you believe in God? How religious are you?

1214. Do you believe in idol worship?

1215. Do you believe in the existence of Satan?

1216. Do you believe in the karma theory?

1217. Do you believe that everything that happens, happens for a reason?

1218. Do you believe that the soul is immortal?

1219. Do you believe that the world was created in six days?

1220. Do you believe the devil exists?

1221. Do you display religious symbols at home?

1222. Do you ever believe in reincarnation? What would you like to be reborn as?

1223. Do you follow and believe religious leaders?

1224. Do you give money to the local church? What motivates you to do so?

1225. Do you like visiting religious places?

1226. Do you say a prayer before your meal?

1227. Do you see a lot of contradictions within any religion and several more between different religions?

1228. Do you think that a marriage between two people belonging to two different religions can succeed?

1229. Do you think all these religious rules are handed down by God, or do you see them as put together by man?

1230. Why do you think so many people are conformists, confirming to what is expected of them by society?

1231. Do you think of the paradoxes in various religions?

1232. Have any of your major decisions in life been shaped by religious considerations?

1233. Have you been drawn to any other religion?

1234. Have you ever been part of a cult?

1235. Have you ever had any reason to turn into an atheist?

1236. Have you ever kept a fast for religious reasons?

1237. Have you studied any religion apart from your own?

1238. Have you studied your own religion?

1239. How do you see people who convert to other religions?

1240. How does your religion see family planning?

1241. How many hours in a week do you spend attending church and/or praying?

1242. How much do you believe in fate and destiny?

1243. How often do you attend church service?

1244. How religious are your parents?

1245. If a couple belongs to different religions, what sort of issues do you think will need to be addressed?

1246. If I turned an atheist and stopped praying, would it affect our relationship in any way?

1247. If you had to opt for marriage counseling who would you trust to mediate between you and your spouse, other than a professional marriage counselor?

1248. If you were in love with someone of a different religion, who insisted that you convert after marriage, would you go ahead with the marriage?

1249. Is it necessary that you have a religious ceremony for your wedding?

1250. Is religion very important to you, when you date someone?

1251. Is there any cult which you're fascinated by?

1252. Is there any religion you don't like, in particular?

1253. Is there any 'spiritual guru' you have?

1254. Is there anything you have done in your life that you consider a major sin?

1255. What aspect of someone's personality - age, wealth, race, religion, would put you off that person, even if you had already fallen for them?

1256. What do you dislike about your religion or disagree with?

1257. What do you like about your own religion?

1258. What do you think happens to us after we die?

1259. What do you think of countries, where laws differ in some aspects for people of different religions?

1260. What do you think of Muslim men who marry several women, taking advantage of their religion?

1261. What do you think of religions such as Islam where women are relegated to a lower status?

1262. What do you think of wars in the name of religion?

1263. What would you like to be in your next birth, assuming that reincarnation is a true theory?

1264. When you pray, what do you thank God for and what do you ask for?

1265. Would you like to be buried or cremated, when you die?

1266. Would you marry an atheist?

58

Romance

1267. Are there any songs you're especially sentimental about?

1268. Are you comfortable with a public display of affection?

1269. Are you sentimental?

1270. Do we have a song that we can consider 'our song'?

1271. Do you kiss on the first date?

1272. Do you like beaches?

1273. Do you like flirting with others?

1274. Do you like men with facial hair or without?

1275. Do you like watching the sunrise or sunset?

1276. Do you like women with long hair or short?

1277. Do you like your partner to touch you frequently?

1278. Do you need your partner to say 'I love you' to you often?

1279. Do you remember our first kiss?

1280. Do you think opposites attract? Would you rather date someone similar or dissimilar to you?

1281. Do you think we have chemistry?

1282. Do you write poetry?

1283. Has anyone ever wooed you ardently?

1284. Has someone ever written poetry for you?

1285. Have you ever been on a blind date?

1286. Have you ever bought lingerie for a partner?

1287. Have you ever tried Internet dating? What was the experience like?

1288. Have you ever written poetry for someone?

1289. Have you saved anything that reminds you of our courtship period?

1290. How frequently do you say 'I love you' to your partner?

1291. How important are anniversaries to you?

1292. How important is it to you that your partner be romantic?

1293. How old were you when someone first confessed their love for you?

1294. How romantic are you?

1295. How would you plan a romantic evening with your partner?

1296. If you could give me a pet name, what would it be?

1297. Tell me about your first kiss.

1298. What does romance mean to you and how important is it?

1299. What has been the most romantic gesture anyone has made for you?

1300. What is the craziest thing you have ever done for someone you love?

1301. What is the most touching gesture anyone has ever made for you?

1302. What is your idea of a romantic holiday?

1303. What is your idea of a romantic meal?

1304. Where would you like to go for your honeymoon?

1305. Which dates do you celebrate in a relationship, the day you met, kissed, made love for the first time…?

1306. Which has been your best date ever?

1307. Which has been your most romantic date?

1308. Which is the most romantic thing you have ever done for anyone?

1309. Which was the first love letter you ever received?

1310. Which was the first love letter you wrote?

59

Self Image

1311. Are you a procrastinator?

1312. Are you camera friendly?

1313. Are you comfortable in your skin?

1314. Are you comfortable with your nude body?

1315. Do you consider yourself a good judge of character?

1316. Do you consider yourself emotionally stable?

1317. Do you consider yourself successful?

1318. Do you feel insecure about anything?

1319. Do you find yourself arrogant at times?

1320. Do you have a pet name? Do you like it?

1321. Do you like your name? Have you ever considered changing it? What would you change it to?

1322. Do you see yourself as worthy of being loved?

1323. Do you think you are a stereotype?

1324. Do you think you are perseverant?

1325. Do you think you are selfish? Why? In which way?

1326. Do you think you are stubborn?

1327. Do you think you have a sense of humor?

1328. Do you think you have double standards - what you do and say are different things sometimes?

1329. Do you think you talk too much, or too little, about yourself?

1330. Do you think you would make a good parent?

1331. Do you think you would make a good spouse?

1332. Do you think you're fat?

1333. How competitive are you?

1334. How do you handle criticism?

1335. How do you think your table manners are?

1336. How far do you think you've grown intellectually, after your formal education was completed?

1337. How frequently do you look into the mirror?

1338. How have you changed as a person, over the years?

1339. How important is it for you to be liked?

1340. How often do you get compliments?

1341. How secure are you as a person?

1342. How strong is your self-esteem?

1343. How would you describe yourself?

1344. If a movie were to be made on your life, what should the title be?

1345. If there was a book on your life, what would it be titled?

1346. If you could be as tall as you wanted to be, how tall would that be?

1347. If you could change anything about the way you look, what would that be?

1348. If you could get plastic surgery done, to change anything about yourself, what would that be?

1349. If you could trade your life with someone else for a day, who would it be? What if it were permanent?

1350. If you had to give yourself a pet name, what would it be?

1351. If you lost a lot of hair and turned semi-bald, what would you do - keep it that way, get a hair-piece, wig or toupee or get a
hair transplant, or maybe shave your head to get a new look?

1352. If you were to write a personal ad about yourself, what would it read?

1353. In which areas do you consider yourself very fortunate?

1354. Is there a picture of yourself, that is your favorite? Why do you like it so much?

1355. Is there any celebrity that you resemble in looks, in your opinion?

1356. Is there anything about your life, which you have a major complex about?

1357. On a scale of one to ten, where you rate yourself when it comes to intelligence?

1358. On a scale of one to ten where do you rate yourself when it comes to looks?

1359. What are your faults?

1360. What do you think is your most attractive feature?

1361. What makes you trustworthy?

1362. When your self-esteem hits a low, do you sometimes do things you wouldn't otherwise?

1363. Which actor do you think you resemble?

1364. Which animal are you like? Do you see yourself as a cunning fox or a vixen, an aggressive lion or a mischievous monkey?

1365. Which are the people whose opinion is important to you?

1366. Which aspect of your personality are you most proud about?

1367. Which character on television, in the movies or from popular books, can you identify with?

1368. Which color do you think represents you best? Why?

1369. Which comic book character would you like to be?

1370. Which has been your wisest decision so far?

1371. Which is the compliment you receive most often?

1372. Which is the most attractive part of the body, for you? Is there any part that you especially like?

1373. Which is the smartest thing you've ever done?

1374. Which of the seven deadly sins - Lust, Gluttony, Greed, Sloth, Wrath, Envy and Pride - do you think you're guilty of?

1375. Which superhero would you like to be?

1376. Would you say you are happy currently, with your life?

60

Sex

1377. Are there any particular fragrances that turn you
on?

1378. Are there any sexual acts that you wouldn't want
your wife to perform with you?

1379. Are there any unusual places in the home where
you would like to have sex - on the kitchen table,
for instance?

1380. Are there sexual fantasies you have, that you
would never want to share with your partner?

1381. Are there times when you have sex only to please
your partner, although you're not in the mood for it?

1382. Are you able to enjoy having sex without having
an orgasm?

1383. Are you bisexual?

1384. Are you comfortable with the idea of having sex
in someone else's home?

1385. Are you into sadomasochism or bondage?

1386. Are you more or less interested in sex today, than you were in the past?

1387. At what age did you attain puberty?

1388. At what age did you discover masturbation? Did you have guilt associated with it?

1389. At what age did you first watch an adult film?

1390. At what age do you think children should be told about sex?

1391. Do you believe you understand the opposite sex, or are they a mystery to you?

1392. Do you discuss sex, in general, with your same-sex friends?

1393. Do you discuss your sexual conquests with your friends?

1394. Do you ever fantasize about someone else when you're having sex with your partner?

1395. Do you expect sex to improve over time in a relationship, or decline as the novelty wears off and predictability makes it boring?

1396. Do you fear losing your sexual virility at some point?

1397. Do you get turned on by porn?

1398. Do you get turned on the most by images, sounds or touch?

1399. Do you have any particular fetish?

1400. Do you have sexual inhibitions?

1401. Do you lie about your sex life when talking with friends?

1402. Do you like cunnilingus and fellatio?

1403. Do you like quickies?

1404. Do you like talking dirty during sex?

1405. Do you like to be mothered by your lover?

1406. Do you like to give massages to your lover, or get massages from them?

1407. Do you like to leave the lights on or switch them off when having sex?

1408. Do you like to look at yourself nude in the mirror?

1409. Do you like to talk when having sex?

1410. Do you like using mirrors to see yourself have sex, when in the act?

1411. Do you like your woman to dress sexy or be covered up?

1412. Do you make noises when having sex?

1413. Do you masturbate? How often?

1414. When you meet someone of the opposite sex that you find attractive, do you mentally strip him/her?

1415. Do you prefer to go slow when having sex, with foreplay and a gradual build-up or do you prefer to just charge ahead?

1416. Do you prefer to keep your pubic hair, trim it or shave it?

1417. Do you prefer to work under a boss of the same sex as you?

1418. Do you remember any sexual experience from childhood? How did it affect you?

1419. Do you remember the first time we made love?

1420. Do you see having sex as being different from making love?

1421. Do you think a man and a woman can have a purely platonic relationship, without even an undercurrent of sexuality?

1422. Do you think discussing sex with your partner can lead to a more fulfilling love life?

1423. Do you think either of us is dominant in bed?

1424. Do you think there is a difference between having sex with someone one is just attracted to, and someone one is in love with?

1425. Do you think it is important for a man and woman to have sex on their wedding night, even if they had a grueling day?

1426. Do you think it is okay for a couple to get counselling if they have a less-than-satisfactory sex life?

1427. Do you think it matters how large the size of a man's penis is?

1428. Do you think it's possible to have too much sex?

1429. Do you think we are sexually compatible?

1430. Do you think working out regularly helps improve sexual performance?

1431. Do you think you could spend your entire life having sex with a single person? Do you think it is realistically possible for you to remain loyal to your partner?

1432. Do you think you have a strong sex drive?

1433. Do you think you have become better between the sheets, over the years?

1434. Do you think you have had as much sex as you would have liked to so far? Would you rather have had more or less?

1435. Do you think you look good naked?

1436. Do you think you're addicted to sex or you could become a sex addict?

1437. Do you think you're passive or aggressive in bed?

1438. Do you think you're very well aware of STD?

1439. Do you think you've become a better lover over the years?

1440. Do you want me to cuddle you more often, without it leading to sex?

1441. For $25,000, would you agree to have sex with someone you barely knew, but who was attracted to you?

1442. Have you even fallen in love with someone you were not attracted to, sexually? Do you think it could happen, if it hasn't?

1443. Have you ever been caught stimulating yourself?

1444. Have you ever been forced into having sex?

1445. Have you ever been paid in cash or kind, to have sex?

1446. Have you ever been part of a sexual orgy?

1447. Have you ever boasted about a sexual conquest that was only in your imagination?

1448. Have you ever faked an orgasm?

1449. Have you ever felt guilty about having sex?

1450. Have you ever forced someone to have sex with you?

1451. Have you ever found yourself attracted to someone of the same sex?

1452. Have you ever got pregnant (for women), or accidentally impregnated someone (for men)?

1453. Have you ever had a one-night-stand?

1454. Have you ever had sex in a public area?

1455. Have you ever had sex in a situation where you were at great risk of having someone walk in?

1456. Have you ever had sex in an unsafe manner, where you were at high risk of being affected by an STD?

1457. Have you ever had sex in the outdoors?

1458. Have you ever had sex with a co-worker?

1459. Have you ever had sex with a friend's partner?

1460. Have you ever had sex with a person you've barely known?

1461. Have you ever had sex with a subordinate at work, implying or promising a favor?

1462. Have you ever had sex in a situation where someone could have walked in on you?

1463. Have you ever had sex with someone of the same sex as you?

1464. Have you ever had sex with someone old enough to be your parent?

1465. Have you ever had sex with someone related to you?

1466. Have you ever had sex with someone who had an STD?

1467. Have you ever had sex with someone who was below the age of consent?

1468. Have you ever had sex with someone, you already knew to be infected with STD?

1469. Have you ever had sex with someone you had no emotional involvement with?

1470. Have you ever had sex with someone young enough to be your kid?

1471. Have you ever had sexual fantasies about someone from the same sex?

1472. Have you ever indulged in mutual masturbation?

1473. Have you ever paid or done a favor for getting sex?

1474. Have you ever photographed, or otherwise captured on camera, your lover in the nude? Have you ever posed nude yourself, on camera, for a lover?

1475. Have you ever read an informative book, to learn about sex?

1476. Have you ever regretted having sex with someone?

1477. Have you ever seduced someone you were sexually attracted to?

1478. Have you ever seen a porn film to learn about sex?

1479. Have you ever taken a bath together with a lover - in the tub or under the shower?

1480. Have you ever told someone you love them, just to have sex with them?

1481. Have you ever tried anal sex?

1482. Have you ever tried morning sex? How do you find it?

1483. Have you ever tried phone sex?

1484. Have you ever tried role-playing during sex?

1485. Have you ever tried sex toys?

1486. Have you ever tried Tantric Sex?

1487. Have you had friends with benefits?

1488. How different is sex with someone you seduce versus sex with someone you're committed or married to, in your opinion?

1489. How do you find oral sex?

1490. How do you find the concept of swapping partners? Would you consider indulging in it?

1491. How do you initiate lovemaking with a partner?

1492. How do you masturbate or stimulate yourself to attain a climax?

1493. How do you react when your partner tells you that they're not in the mood to have sex?

1494. How do you think sex changes after a couple has been married for several years, or after having children?

1495. How do you think the sex life of a couple changes over time?

1496. How important do you think foreplay is to sex?

1497. How important do you think sex is?

1498. How important is sex to you?

1499. How long do you think foreplay should last?

1500. How long does your average sexual encounter last?

1501. How many people have you had sex with?

1502. How many times a day, do you find yourself thinking about sex?

1503. How many times a day do you think about sex?

1504. How often are you able to have an orgasm, when you have sex?

1505. How often have you given an excuse, to avoid having sex?

1506. How often have you had sex on the first date?

1507. How often would you like to have sex? Do you currently have sex more or less often than you would like to?

1508. How old were you when you first saw a person of the opposite sex, nude?

1509. How old were you, when you found out about the birds and the bees?

1510. How old were you, when you lost your virginity?

1511. How old would your children have to be, before you discuss sex with them?

1512. How would it affect you if you had to initiate sex most times, rather than your partner?

1513. How would you rate yourself as a lover?

1514. How would you react, if you found out your partner was bisexual?

1515. If a couple is in love with each other, but don't have much sexual chemistry, how do you think they should deal with it?

1516. If either of us lost interest in sex, do you think our relationship would still survive?

1517. If either of us lost the ability to enjoy sex, how would it affect our relationship?

1518. If I had a friend of the opposite sex who was very attractive, would you be concerned if we spent a lot of time together?

1519. If I put on a lot of weight, would you lose interest in having sex with me?

1520. If I told you that I had some sexual fantasies I wanted to try out, would you be willing?

1521. If there were a fool-proof protection against all STDs, would you have sex with multiple partners?

1522. If we had a less-than-satisfactory sex life, would you be open to consulting a sex therapist who could help us enhance it?

1523. If you could have sex with any one person you chose, who would that be?

1524. If you dated someone and they were very bad in bed, would you talk about it to friends?

1525. If you discovered that someone you were very much in love with, had a checkered past with a string of lovers, would it make a difference to you?

1526. If you found out that the person you're married to had, at some point, granted sexual favors to retain a job, how would you react?

1527. If you had to choose between a very wealthy existence but with no sex life at all (like marrying a rich man who's incapable of having sex), or having a life where you could have very satisfying sex with several lovers, but barely enough money to make ends meet, which life would you choose?

1528. If you have a sexual problem, who are you most likely to talk to?

1529. If you want to have sex, but your partner isn't in the mood, how do you deal with it?

1530. If you were rendered sexually inactive temporarily, for some reason, do you think you could trust your partner to remain loyal to you?

1531. If your man ejaculated too quickly and left you dissatisfied, what would you do?

1532. If your partner had a much lower or much higher sex drive than yours, how would you deal with it?

1533. If your partner put on a lot of weight, do you think it would affect your sex life?

1534. If your partner was unable to satisfy you, at what point would you seek sex outside the relationship?

1535. Is it advantageous to have sex with a person before you marry them?

1536. Is it easy for you to talk to your lover about what turns you on or what turns you off?

1537. Is it important to you to have at least one child of each sex?

1538. Is it usually you or your partner who initiates sex?

1539. Is there any aphrodisiac that you have found to be very effective?

1540. Is there any celebrity you would want to have sex with?

1541. Is there any part of the anatomy of the opposite sex, that you find particularly attractive?

1542. Is there any particular music that turns you on?

1543. Is there any sexual activity that you would want to try, but are afraid to?

1544. Is there anything about sex that makes you awkward or uncomfortable?

1545. Is there anything missing from your sex life, that could make it more fulfilling?

1546. Is there someone from the past who you would want to locate and seduce?

1547. Should sex only be for procreation?

1548. Some people continue to masturbate despite having an active sex life. Why do you think this is so?

1549. What attracts you sexually, in a person?

1550. What do you notice first when you meet someone of the opposite sex?

1551. What do you think about abstaining from sex until marriage and then practicing monogamy?

1552. What do you think of cultures, where virginity is considered sacred and to be preserved until marriage?

1553. What do you think of making love outdoors?

1554. What do you think of people who like to be dominated or spanked by their partners, during the act?

1555. What do you think of people who use sex as a tool to get their way in the marriage?

1556. What do you think of sexting? Have you ever sent nude pictures of yourself to someone else?

1557. What do you think of women with smaller breasts, who opt for surgery to enlarge them?

1558. What do you think should be the age of consent for sex?

1559. What if you could never have sex again?

1560. What is it about the opposite sex, that you can never understand?

1561. What is the biggest turn-on for you when having sex?

1562. What is the longest that a lovemaking session has lasted, for you?

1563. What is the longest period you've gone without having sex, after you became sexually active?

1564. What is the longest you have ever waited, to have sex with someone you were in a relationship with?

1565. What is the most sexually adventurous thing you've done?

1566. What is your earliest memory, of being sexually aware?

1567. What is your favorite position when having sex?

1568. What is your favorite sexual fantasy?

1569. What makes you feel sexy?

1570. What misconceptions did you have about sex, during your childhood?

1571. What percentage of adults do you think are satisfied sexually?

1572. What percentage of adults do you think are virgins?

1573. What sort of contraception do you prefer?

1574. What sort of inner wear would you like your lover to wear? Have you ever bought inner wear for a lover?

1575. What turns you off completely, when you're having sex?

1576. What would you do, if your partner forced you to have sex with them against your wishes?

1577. What you think of people, who need to suffer pain to enjoy sex?

1578. What's the maximum number of times you've had sex within a single day?

1579. When drunk, have you ever had sex with someone you wouldn't normally have been intimate with?

1580. When we have sex, is there anything I do, that you especially like?

1581. When we have sex, is there anything I do that you would rather I did less of or didn't do?

1582. When you have sex, is it more important to derive pleasure for yourself, or to please your partner?

1583. When you meet someone attractive, do you fantasize about how it would be to have sex with them?

1584. Which is the most unusual place at which you had sex?

1585. Which is the one sexual act that is unthinkable for you?

1586. Which is the part of body of the opposite sex that you find the most unattractive?

1587. Which is your preferred method of birth control?

1588. Which is your favorite time of the day to have sex?

1589. Which is your wildest sexual fantasy?

1590. Which part of your personality do you use the most, to attract the opposite sex?

1591. Which parts of your anatomy are more sensitive to touch?

1592. Which trait in the opposite sex do you dislike?

1593. Which would you consider your most memorable sexual experience, so far?

1594. Who was the first person you had sex with? What was the experience like?

1595. Who was the first person you were sexually attracted to? How did you deal with this?

1596. Would it bother you if I told you I have had several sexual partners in the past? Would you want to know all about it?

1597. Would it bother you if I walked around the house naked?

1598. Would you agree to sleep with someone, if you were assured a promotion you were looking forward to? What if it were someone of the same sex?

1599. Would you be okay with your partner having a close friend of the opposite sex? What if you were assured that the relationship was purely platonic?

1600. Would you consider cybersex to be cheating?

1601. Would you get yourself tested for STD, if I asked you to?

1602. Would you rather have an experienced lover or a virgin?

1603. What would you think of people who use sex as a tool, to get their way in the marriage?

61

Shopping

1604. Are you a compulsive shopper?

1605. Do you cut out or collect coupons or search for codes on the internet, that will save you money when shopping?

1606. Do you like going shopping with your partner? Why, or why not?

1607. Do you like shopping at discount sales?

1608. Do you like shopping?

1609. Do you like to wear clothes that show off your body?

1610. Do you like trying new clothes, or is it a chore?

1611. Does buying new clothes or shopping for gadgets and other things you covet, boost your self image?

1612. Have you ever bought something you really regret?

1613. How many pairs of shoes do you own?

1614. How much do you spend on clothes every month?

1615. How often do you go shopping for clothes?

1616. What sort of clothing do you like to wear, to feel attractive and sexy?

62

Sleeping

1617. Are you able to fall asleep with the lights on?

1618. Are you able to sleep, if your immediate environment is messy, or has a lot of clutter?

1619. Can you sleep in a bed that hasn't been made?

1620. Do you snore in your sleep?

1621. Do you suffer from insomnia?

1622. How many hours a day do you sleep? Given a choice, would you want to sleep longer every day?

1623. If you could get by with an hour of sleep every day, how would you use the extra time?

1624. If you wake up two hours earlier than usual, do you get out of bed, or make an attempt to sleep again?

1625. Is it easy for you get sleep?

1626. What if you married someone who was used to sleeping much later or earlier, than the time at which you retired for the day?

63

Spirituality and New Age

1627. Do you have any spiritual goals? How do you plan to attain them?

1628. Do you think you have a sixth sense?

1629. Have you ever got Feng Shui done?

1630. Have you ever got your birth chart analyzed by an astrologer? What have they said about you?

1631. Have you ever got your palm read?

1632. Have you ever had a 'déjà vu' experience?

1633. Have you ever had a premonition?

1634. Have you ever had a psychic experience?

1635. Have you ever had an out-of-body experience?

1636. Have you ever used the ouija board?

1637. Have you ever visited a Psychic?

1638. What is your Feng Shui Pa Kua number?

1639. What is your Sun Sign as per astrology?

64

Sports

1640. Are there any sports events that you never miss?

1641. Are you into cycling?

1642. Do you know how to roller skate?

1643. Do you know skiing?

1644. Do you like adventure sports?

1645. Do you like boating or sailing?

1646. Do you play cricket or baseball?

1647. Do you play golf?

1648. Have you tried bungee jumping?

1649. Have you tried scuba diving?

1650. How involved are you when watching a sports event? Do you get disappointed when the side you're backing loses?

65

Talents and Skills

1651. Are there any foreign languages that you speak?

1652. Are you good with numbers and calculations?

1653. Are you handy at fixing things around the house?

1654. Are you quick at picking up new things?

1655. Can you dance?

1656. Can you sing?

1657. Can you swim?

1658. Do you have a talent for mechanics?

1659. Do you know carpentry?

1660. Do you know horse riding?

1661. Do you know how to ride the bicycle?

1662. Have you ever tried writing?

1663. How creative are you?

1664. How is your sense of direction?

1665. Is there any musical instrument you can play?

1666. Is there any talent you really wish you had?

1667. Which are your talents?

1668. Which of your talents or qualities, do you like to be acknowledged by others?

66

Technology

1669. Are you able to cope with new technologies and gizmos easily?

1670. Are you fond of gizmos and tech gadgets?

1671. Do you think, technology such as mobile phones and the internet, have made it impossible for us to relax?

1672. Do you visit internet chat rooms?

1673. Does technology intimidate you?

1674. Have you signed up with Orkut, Twitter or Facebook?

1675. How often do you change your mobile phone?

1676. Would you have preferred to be part of an era where technology didn't play such an important role?

67

Temperament

1677. After you lose your temper, how long does it take you to come back to a normal state? Do you spend days sulking?

1678. Are you a good loser?

1679. Are you a perfectionist?

1680. Are you able to handle an emergency or crisis well?

1681. Are you an analytical person, or do you go by how you feel about a situation?

1682. Are you an emotional person?

1683. Are you an optimist or a pessimist?

1684. Are you childish in any aspect of your life?

1685. Are you good at keeping secrets?

1686. Are you short tempered?

1687. Are you susceptible to road rage?

1688. Do people often take you for a ride?

1689. Do you cry easily?

1690. Do you cry when you watch a sentimental movie?

1691. Do you ever feel lonely?

1692. Do you find yourself envious or jealous of people who're more successful than you?

1693. Do you have any prejudices?

1694. Do you like to eavesdrop on conversations?

1695. Do you like to listen to music when working? What sort of music?

1696. Do you remember significant dates, when you're in a relationship, such as the day you met, the first time you kissed, or made love?

1697. Do you tend to exaggerate?

1698. Do you think you tend to dominate, in a relationship?

1699. Do you think you're a disciplined person? In which ways are you disciplined, or not?

1700. Have you ever come close to a nervous breakdown?

1701. Have you ever come close to slipping into depression?

1702. Have you ever suffered from an inferiority complex, or otherwise felt very inferior to someone?

1703. Have you ever wanted to take revenge for something?

1704. How does stress affect you?

1705. How much privacy do you need?

1706. How patient are you?

1707. How rigid are you? Are you likely to change your mind quickly, or does it take a lot for you to budge?

1708. If someone points out a fault, do you generally accept it, or get defensive?

1709. If you're stuck in a task, are you more likely to ask for help, or continue to struggle on your own?

1710. Is it easy for you to say 'no' to people?

1711. Is there any subject you are particularly touchy about?

1712. What are you like, when you're depressed or sad?

1713. What are you like, when you're happy?

1714. What do you think of people who strive for perfection in their work?

1715. What makes you sad?

1716. When was the last time you cried?

1717. When you are in a bad mood, how do you like others to deal with you?

1718. When you feel low, what do you do to get your spirits up?

1719. Would you consider yourself an extrovert or an introvert?

68

The Past

1720. Are there any crucial decisions in your life that you have taken and that you now regret?

1721. Do I remind you of anyone from the present or the past?

1722. Do you keep pictures and memorabilia of past lovers?

1723. Do you often find yourself living in, and dwelling on, the past?

1724. Do you regret any of your relationships?

1725. Do you think if someone spoke to your exes about you, they would speak well, or ill, about you?

1726. Does the past weigh heavy on you or are you easily able to let it go?

1727. Have you ever been engaged? What went wrong?

1728. Have you ever been so wronged by a partner, that you considered taking revenge?

1729. Have you ever broken up with someone and then gone back to them? Who had initiated the break-up? Was your relationship better or worse, the second time around?

1730. Have you ever felt very strongly about a relationship you were in, expecting it to last forever? How many times has this happened?

1731. Have you ever gone hungry?

1732. Have you ever met an ex after a gap of several years? What was it like?

1733. Have you met anyone with whom you had lost touch a long time ago?

1734. How did you find them?

1735. How do people from the past react, when they meet you?

1736. How do your friends and associates from long ago, react when they meet you? Do they think you've changed?

1737. If my ex made a constant effort to stay in touch with me, would it bother you?

1738. If there is any one day of your life that you could live all over again, which would that be?

1739. If you could go back and change any significant decision you took, which one would that be?

1740. If you could relive your life all over again, what would you do differently?

1741. If you discovered a one-night-stand of your spouse, that took place many years ago, how would you deal with it?

1742. If you had been able to spend your entire life with your first love, do you think you would've had a successful relationship?

1743. Is there anyone in your life, that you can never forgive? Where did they go wrong?

1744. Is there anyone you would never want to see again? What have they done, to cause such a strong feeling?

1745. Is there anything about your past that I should know?

1746. Is there anything in your past, that you would want to do your best to cover up?

1747. Is there anything you've said to someone, that you wish you had never said?

1748. Is there someone from your past, who you have still not got over?

1749. What has been the reason for your relationships to end, in the past?

1750. What have been the turning points in your life?

1751. What mistakes do you think you have made, in your past relationships?

1752. Which negative qualities about you, would your exes talk about, if someone asked them?

1753. Which was your last relationship? How long did it last and what went wrong?

1754. Who is the one person you're no longer in touch with, who you miss the most?

1755. Would you meet a past lover, even if you knew I didn't approve?

69

Traveling

1756. Have you ever been to a safari park?

1757. If you won a 10-day all-expense-paid trip to anywhere in the world, where would you head?

1758. Which are the places you have traveled to?

70

Trust

1759. How long does it take, for you to really trust someone?

1760. How often do you lie? What do you usually lie about?

1761. If someone breaks your trust, are you able to trust the person again? Does it take a long time?

1762. What makes a person trustworthy?

71

Vacations

1763. Do you fly economy class or business class?

1764. Do you go someplace, which is a day's drive away, to relax?

1765. Do you like sun-bathing?

1766. Do you like the process of traveling or would you rather reach your destination as early as you can?

1767. Do you like to plan ahead of time, or do you take off on impulse?

1768. Do you like traveling?

1769. Do you need a lot of amenities when you're traveling?

1770. Do you prefer traveling alone, with family or friends?

1771. Do you prefer visiting countries that have historical significance, or would you rather go to places with religious significance, or those with picturesque locales?

1772. Do you read about the places you're traveling to, before you go there?

1773. Do you report ahead of time at the airport, or is it generally at the last moment?

1774. Do you research the travel destination, before you go there?

1775. Do you take a lot of stuff with you when you travel?

1776. Have you ever been on a luxury cruise?

1777. Have you ever thought about owning a vacation home?

1778. Have you thought of taking a sabbatical?

1779. How do you finance your vacations? Is it out of your savings, or do you run up a credit card debt?

1780. How do you interact with people, who don't understand your language, when you're traveling?

1781. How long are your holiday breaks, generally?

1782. How many weeks a year can you give to traveling?

1783. How much do your holidays generally end up costing?

1784. How often do you travel? Is it for work or pleasure?

1785. On a tour, do you prefer traveling alone, with friends, family, or in a group?

1786. On a vacation, do you prefer sightseeing, or lazing around and relaxing?

1787. What would a perfect vacation be like for you?

1788. When did you first travel by air?

1789. When was the last time you took off on a holiday?

1790. When you go traveling, do you like to rough it out or do you expect luxury?

1791. Which is the time of the year, when you like to travel?

1792. Which is your favorite holiday destination?

1793. Who looks after your home, when you're on a holiday?

1794. Are your vacations only for pleasure or are they business-cum-pleasure trips?

1795. Do you get air-sick or sea-sick?

1796. How many vacations a year do you think we would take, when we're married?

1797. Which has been your most memorable holiday?

72

Work and Career

1798. Are you a team worker, or do you prefer working alone?

1799. Are you in the career you qualified for? If not, why did you choose a different career?

1800. Are you satisfied with the rate of growth in your career?

1801. Are you usually a victim of office politics, or are you the one getting the better of others?

1802. At what stage of life would you like to retire?

1803. At your workplace, have there been any instances of your co-workers taking credit for work that you have done?

1804. Do you experience politics at your workplace?

1805. Do you feel secure in your current job?

1806. Do you have a killer instinct in your work?

1807. Do you have to entertain business acquaintances regularly?

1808. Do you like your boss?

1809. Do you suffer from Monday blues?

1810. Do you take pride in your work?

1811. Do you take work home?

1812. Do you think people respect you enough, for your professional achievements? Do you think you deserve more respect than you get?

1813. Do you think you chose your career wisely?

1814. Do you think you work harder than most other people who work with you?

1815. Do you think you're a workaholic?

1816. Does your job require late hours or working on holidays?

1817. For twice your current pay, would you be willing to spend two years working in a one-horse town away from most facilities?

1818. Has someone else ever beaten you to a promotion, unfairly?

1819. Have any of your co-workers ever tried to seduce you?

1820. Have you ever asked for a raise? Were you successful in getting it?

1821. Have you ever been fired? How did you cope with it?

1822. Have you ever been mentored by anyone?

1823. Have you ever been passed over for a promotion that you were due for? How did you deal with it?

1824. Have you ever considered relocating?

1825. Have you ever gone to your boss for a raise? Did you get it?

1826. Have you ever lied at a job interview, or fudged your resume to make it more attractive?

1827. Have you ever run a business?

1828. Have you ever tried to seduce a co-worker?

1829. Have you ever wanted to start something of your own? What has held you back?

1830. How do you define success?

1831. How do you spend your time at work, when you don't have much work to do?

1832. How frequently do you call in sick at work, just to take a day off?

1833. How friendly are you with your co-workers?

1834. How many hours a week do you work?

1835. Do you wish you could work more hours, or less hours than you currently do?

1836. How much money do you think you'll be making in your career, five years from now?

1837. How often do you call in sick, when you're not really so?

1838. How secure do you think your current job is?

1839. How would you like to spend your life post-retirement?

1840. If I had to live in a different city for two years, due to a career development, would you move with me? Would you prefer we lived apart for the two years?

1841. If you could change your career, which vocation would you take up?

1842. If you could take a year off and not have to work, how would you spend the year?

1843. If you could take up a career which brought you less money, but left you with more free time to travel, would you consider it?

1844. If you don't like your boss, have you had bosses you've liked? What were they like?

1845. If you had choose, between a job that was very well paying, but left you with no time for family, and one that paid reasonably well and would let you see more of your family, which one would you pick?

1846. If you had to change your career, which are the talents you could use to make money?

1847. If you had to give up your current career, which other talents could you use to make a living?

1848. If you lost your job today, what would you do?

1849. If you're having a lean day at work, how do you spend your free time?

1850. What are the near term, medium term and long term goals in your career?

1851. What made you get into the career you've chosen?

1852. What would the perfect job be for you?

1853. Where do you see yourself in your career, five years from now?

1854. Which are the professions you considered taking up as a child or teen?

1855. Which has been your best job so far?

1856. Which has been your longest employment so far? Which was the shortest?

1857. Which is the biggest career risk you have taken?

1858. Which was your first job?

1859. Which was your worst boss?

1860. Who do you list as your references?

1861. Would you change your career or your country of residence, for someone you loved?

1862. Would you ever consider retiring to a small town or maybe the countryside?

1863. Would you ever consider starting a business with your spouse?

1864. Would you take up a job that required you to travel extensively throughout the country?

1865. Would you work extra hours on your job, without being given extra compensation for it?

1866. Would you work the graveyard shift instead, if it meant a 30% increase in your pay?

73

Ethical Questions

1867. You're at a large department store, where you find a woman stuffing a box of chocolates into her shirt. It's clear she's not going to be caught. Would you stop her, or bring it to the notice of the store, or just ignore it and go about your own shopping?

1868. A cabbie returns you $20 more in change than was due to you. Would you give it back?

1869. You try to withdraw $100 from the ATM, but get $300 instead. Would you report it to the bank?

1870. Would you kill a chicken with a sharp knife by beheading it, if you were offered $500 to do so?

1871. From a natural disaster, if you could rescue either a 3-year-old child or a nuclear scientist important to your country, who would you rescue?

1872. You get a $50 bill at the supermarket, that you realize later, is fake. It looks very much like the real thing, but your cousin, who works for a bank, tells you it's a fake. Would you report it to the authorities, destroy it, or spend it at the earliest?

1873. A close friend's wife asks you to come over to help her with some house repair. When you go to her house, she makes advances at you. You know that your friend is traveling and will never find out.

Your wife trusts you completely. There's no risk of being discovered and you've always found your friend's wife attractive. Would you have sex with her?

1874. You head the legal ministry of your country. A plane is hijacked and the hijackers want five terrorists who have been caught after years of pursuit, to be released. If you don't release the terrorists, the hijackers threaten to blow up the plane and at least 200 innocent people will die. You know that these five terrorists will almost certainly get a death sentence shortly. If released, they will probably cause the death of hundreds or even thousands of people in the future. You have the final authority to decide. What would you do?

1875. You're the vice president of sales of a major chain of departmental stores. Your company stocks branded apparel that stops selling at the end of every season. You're asked to dispose these branded clothes by cutting them into pieces so they can't be used by anyone. The big companies want to protect their brand image and don't want their apparel to end up on street children. Yet you know that winter is around the corner and many of these homeless will freeze to death. They could use these clothes. You won't lose any money either way but these companies will be very upset if you don't do this and you could jeopardize your business relationships. What would you do?

74

More on Relatives

Tick which of these applies to you:

1876. I intend staying in touch with only close relatives.

1877. It's impossible to meet everyone. If I did that, it's all I'll ever be doing.

1878. I would loan money to a relative, if asked to.

1879. I don't believe in taking money from, or giving loans to relatives

1880. Relatives are pests.

1881. It's important for me to stay in touch with all my relatives. They're family, after all.

1882. I would be open to relatives coming over and staying with us for a few days.

1883. When I ask relatives to come and visit us, I really mean it.

1884. I like attending birthdays, marriages and other celebrations of relatives. If I can't make it, I usually send a gift.

1885. If I ran a business and there was scope to hire someone, I would consider hiring a relative.

75

More on Friends

Tick the ones that apply to you:

1886. I stay in touch with all my friends.

1887. I usually only call friends up on their birthdays.

1888. I would want to have more friends than I do.

1889. I approve of my partner's friends.

1890. I don't like some of my partner's friends, but there's little I can do.

1891. My partner spends too much time with friends.

1892. I don't like my partner spending too much time with friends of the opposite sex.

1893. It's hard to stay in touch with your friends, once you're married and have a busy career.

1894. Most of my friends are single.

76

Living together

If you're planning to live in together, these are some important questions:

    1895. Will either of you be cooking, or will you be getting TV dinners/ ordering in?

    1896. Who will be washing the dishes?

    1897. Who will do the laundry?

    1898. Who will dust and vacuum the house?

    1899. How will you split expenses, including the house rent and electricity?

    1900. Who'll make the bed?

    1901. Who will go shopping for groceries and everyday necessities?

    1902. Who'll do the yard work and mow the lawn?

    1903. How will you share the TV?

1904. Who's going to stay at home, when there is a need to?

77

Things that bother you..

Does any of this bother or irritate you?

1905. A wet bathroom floor

1906. Builder's bums

1907. Chauvinistic men

1908. Cruelty to animals

1909. Cyclists on the wrong side of the road

1910. Drivers who weave in and out of heavy traffic

1911. Eavesdropping

1912. Feminists

1913. Flat soda or beer

1914. Free trial offers that come with fine print

1915. Getting a tie or a bottle of perfume as a birthday gift

1916. Girls who use too much war paint

1917. Gossiping

1918. Having to interact with technical support personnel

1919. Hidden costs in financial products

1920. Know-it-alls

1921. Leaving hair in the sink

1922. Men who makes jokes about women and PMS

1923. Men who stare at women, like they've never seen one before

1924. Mother-in-law jokes

1925. Movie sequels of films

1926. Movies with corny story lines

1927. Narcissistic people

1928. Noisy children

1929. Nosy people

1930. Not leaving the toilet seat up

1931. Off-color jokes, dark humor or sick jokes

1932. Opinionated people

1933. Overpriced mineral water at restaurants

1934. People chewing with their mouth open

1935. People distracted by their mobile phone while they're talking to you?

1936. People talking with their mouth full

1937. People who always seem to talk in a patronizing tone

1938. People who are always exaggerating

1939. People who are not serious about their career

1940. People who are overly suspicious of everyone and everything

1941. People who ask needless questions

1942. People who ask you for your frank opinion, but only want an endorsement of their own.

1943. People who behave like over-grown, pampered children

1944. People who bombard your email box with forwards.

1945. People who borrow books and then don't return them

1946. People who brag about themselves

1947. People who can never be punctual

1948. People who can never make up their mind about anything

1949. People who can't control their dogs

1950. People who can't spell to save their life

1951. People who can't talk without cussing

1952. People who claim to read, but never get beyond TV guides and comics

1953. People who don't bathe everyday

1954. People who don't call back

1955. People who don't look at you, when they're talking to you

1956. People who don't wash their hands, after using the wash room

1957. People who doubt everything

1958. People who drink too much

1959. People who get nostalgic at the drop of a hat

1960. People who have conspiracy theories for everything

1961. People who have toddlers in their laps when they drive

1962. People who indulge in baby talk

1963. People who insist on showing you their home videos or picture albums

1964. People who let their pets poop anywhere and never clean up

1965. People who litter everywhere they go

1966. People who make you talk to their toddlers on the phone

1967. People who mispronounce your name

1968. People who never thank anyone for anything

1969. People who never vote

1970. People who nudge you, when your eyes are closed, to ask if you're sleeping

1971. People who offer unasked-for advice

1972. People who over-react to everything

1973. People who play music at very high decibels

1974. People who procrastinate

1975. People who refuse to dress their age

1976. People who repeat the same jokes or anecdotes for years

1977. People who send you email in all caps

1978. People who send you too many text messages because they're on a free SMS plan

1979. People who slurp noisily when they drink a hot beverage

1980. People who sneeze and cough in your face

1981. People who spend most of their waking hours sending and receiving text messages on their cell phone

1982. People who talk about themselves in the third person

1983. People who talk far too much

1984. People who talk so loudly on the phone, that you have to stop all conversation around them

1985. People who try to finish your sentences

1986. People who use the cell phone when driving

1987. People who use too much business jargon

1988. People who want to sing or dance at every opportunity

1989. People who waste food

1990. People who wear the same pair of socks for days on end

1991. People who will do anything for attention

1992. People who won't dress for their body type

1993. People who're always asking for favors

1994. People who're always complaining

1995. People who're always trying to borrow money

1996. People who're always trying to borrow something

1997. People who're always whining about needing to lose weight but who never do anything about it

1998. People who're ardent fans and will argue on behalf of their favorite actor

1999. People who're blatantly selfish

2000. People who're obsessed with their little children and can't stop talking about them

2001. People who're very warm when they meet you, but don't really give a damn

2002. People with a strong racial bias

2003. People with body odor who refuse to use deodorants

2004. People with poor driving skills

2005. People with strong biases

2006. People with vocabularies that can fit on a post card

2007. Picking noses in public

2008. Poor listeners

2009. Pseudo intellectuals

2010. Shopaholics

2011. Smokers who don't respect the space of non-smokers

2012. Snoring

2013. Soap pieces on the bathroom floor

2014. Spam – unsolicited email for everything, from hair loss to sexual health pills and weight loss programs

2015. Spelling mistakes in mail you receive

2016. Tailgating drivers

2017. Telemarketing phone calls

2018. Vain people

******

About the Author

Vikram Chandiramani is the editor of Futurescopes.com, a website that focuses on dating and relationship advice and horoscopes. He also runs Parinda.com, a news website. The official website of this book is www.tellmehoney.com . This is where you can buy copies of this book to gift your friends and join the mailing list to stay informed about books written by the author.

You can reach the author via email at vikram@tellmehoney.com .

Snail Mail:

VMC Infotech
222/ Shantivan,
New Link Rd. Extn.,
Andheri West
Mumbai 53, India
Tel: 91-22-66996298
Fax: 91-22-26350503

LaVergne, TN USA
02 November 2010
203297LV00004B/125/P